THE
Cookbook

A Historical View of Cooking, Traveling and Surviving on the Trail

This cookbook is a collection of 370 recipes and remedies, some dating back to the era of the Oregon Trail. Some recipes were included in this cookbook for the purpose of historical value and are not intended to be prepared, unless you enjoy cooking over buffalo chips! However, you will find modern day versions of Dutch oven cooking, wild game, canning, pickling and handed down ethnic recipes from immigrants who traveled the trail. We hope you enjoy this insightful and unique cookbook!

Additional copies of the Oregon Trail Cookbook may be obtained by sending a check for $10.95 plus $2.00 for shipping/handling to the address below. For your convenience, order blanks are included in the back of this book.

Morris Publishing
P. O. Box 233
Kearney, NE 68848

Retail outlets may obtain the Oregon Trail Cookbook at special rates. Write to the above address for more information.

William Henry Jackson watercolors courtesy of Scotts Bluff National Monument.
Editors: Tamara Omtvedt & Kirsten Bespalec
Publisher: Scott Morris

Library of Congress Catalog Card Number 93-078500
ISBN 0-9631249-3-5

Printed in the U.S.A. by:
Morris Publishing
3212 E. Hwy 30
Kearney, NE 68847
(308) 236-7888

BIBLIOGRAPHY:
Driggs, Howard R., THE OLD WEST SPEAKS. Englewood Cliffs, NJ, Prentice Hall, Inc., 1956.
Dunlop, Richard, GREAT TRAILS OF THE WEST. Nashville, TN, Parthenon Press, 1971.
FOXFIRE BOOK, THE. Anchor Books, Garden City, NY, Anchor Press/Doubleday, 1972.
FOXFIRE 2. Anchor Books, Garden City, NY, Anchor Press/Doubleday, 1972.
Horn, Huston, THE PIONEERS. New York, NY, Time-Life Inc., 1974.
Marcy, Randolph B., THE PRAIRIE TRAVELER: A HAND-BOOK FOR OVERLAND EXPEDITIONS. New York, NY, Harper & Brothers Publishers, 1859.
STORY OF THE GREAT AMERICAN WEST. The Reader's Digest Association, Inc., Pleasantville, New York, 1977.
TRAILS WEST. Special Publications Division, Washington, D.C., National Geographic Society, 1979.

TABLE OF CONTENTS

ABOUT THE ARTIST

William Henry Jackson
1843-1942

The paintings on the cover, dividers and history pages are the work of photographer/artist, William Henry Jackson.

Born in 1843, in the state of New York, William Henry Jackson was a self-taught artist. He began his photography career at the age of 15, working as a retoucher in a photographer's studio. Several years later he went to work for a studio in Vermont, only to leave, enlisting in the Union Army at the outset of the Civil War.

In 1866 Jackson followed the advice of Horace Greeley and headed west. In Nebraska City, one of the earliest Nebraska towns, he worked as a bullwhacker for a freighting outfit, bound for the goldfields of Montana. Traveling along the old Oregon Trail, Jackson sketched the landmarks, sites and hardships experienced by westward bound emigrants. Upon returning, he opened a photography studio in Omaha, Nebraska.

At a time when most men consider retiring, Jackson took on new interests, careers, and even set out for a world tour. At the age of 92, Jackson was asked by the Director of the National Park Service to paint four murals for the new Department of the Interior building in Washington, D.C.

Jackson died two months after celebrating his 99th birthday in 1942. Throughout his long life, Jackson witnessed and captured many changes in American life through his camera lens and paintings.

Renowned for his photography, his paintings portray the immense and diverse talent of this explorer. From those early sketches, often made upon the spot and realized with painstaking accuracy, Jackson created his watercolors depicting paths, hardships and everyday life along the trail. His work has preserved a vital part of our history.

Today, a wing of the Visitor Center at the Scotts Bluff National Monument in Gering, Nebraska contains a large number of his original paintings. Our thanks to the Scotts Bluff National Monument for graciously allowing us to use the watercolors found in this cookbook.

OREGON TRAIL HISTORY

Beginnings,
hardships,
crossings,
forts,
and the
people.

COUNCIL BETWEEN WHITES AND INDIANS

The Indians blazed many trails across the United States, one of which became the Oregon Trail; they called it Big Medicine Trail. The trail climbed from the Great Plains through a break in the Rockies in south Wyoming, which the pioneers called South Pass. The trail then followed the North Platte and Sweetwater Rivers across the Great Divide, passed through the Green River Valley, around the Wasatch Mountains and traced the Bear and Snake Rivers into Hell's Canyon. There it turned northwest over the plateaus and valleys to the Columbia River, which descended into the Pacific. White explorers and mountain men traveled the Big Medicine Trail west, but its name is recorded in history as the Oregon Trail.

OREGON TRAIL HISTORY

Long before the Oregon Trail was traveled by wagon, the region of Oregon had been reached by water routes charted by explorers and fur traders. The long trail from the East across an untamed region first traveled by buffalo and Indians, did not become a road for covered wagons until 30 years later.

It was Joe Meek, a mountain man from Virginia, who in 1840, first proved that wagons could be driven across the prairie grass, sand and mountains into the Columbia River Valley.

In 1843, the "Great Migration" headed West in search of the "pioneer's paradise" promised by those who had already experienced the Pacific Northwest. The Oregon Trail was no great superhighway across the continent, but simply a pair of parallel ruts across a desolate prairie, rocky mountain passes and sandy western deserts.❖

OREGON TRAIL HISTORY

WHY GO WEST?

The hope of promise and undeniable curiosity led many settlers across a wilderness trail that was originally traveled by Indians, and later followed by fur traders, trappers and missionaries. The West promised something better--richer soil, bluer skies, a brighter future and a challenge to be met. The American quest for better opportunities and more room could not be squelched by reports of a bleak prairie desert or perilous mountains.

Other, more tangible reasons also motivated families to venture across an unknown land. In the Northeast, opposition to black slavery prompted many to choose the unsettled and unmarred West. The financial collapse in 1837, which caused New York banks to close their doors and agricultural prices to drop, provided farmers with enough reason to look for better opportunities. Visions of blue skies and clean air moved city dwellers plagued by epidemics such as typhoid, dysentery and cholera to seek a healthier life out West.

> **66 On the 21st of May. . . we arrived in the town of Independence, Missouri. Our destination was the Oregon Territory.** Some of our number sought health in the wilderness--others sought the wilderness for its own sake--and others sought a residence among the ancient forests and lofty heights of the valley of the Columbia. **99**
>
> ~ Thomas Farnham, 1839, Missouri

"Emigrants" as they were called, was a 19th century name for the pioneers. They were in a very real sense emigrants; leaving their own familiar country and going out into a land that was foreign and uncivilized.

Most of the pioneers were American born. They were not necessarily rich; in fact, many hoped to escape economic hardship. However, neither were they without funds, as it cost from $700 to $1,500 to outfit a family for the trip. They were innocent and did not know of the hazards that lay ahead, but they met the perils with courage and settled the West.❖

OREGON TRAIL HISTORY

WAGONS AS FAR AS THE EYE CAN SEE

The Oregon Trail remained in use from the early 1830's until the completion of the trans-continental railroad in 1869. Some pioneers and freighters continued to use the trail into the 1880's, but by then, the days of mass migration by wagon train were over.

In 1841 the first wagon train party, the Bidwell-Bartelson party comprised of 69 travelers, reached the Snake River before abandoning their wagons and completing the journey on foot with pack animals. The following year approximately 200 more pioneers braved the trip. In 1843, the year of the "Great Migration", Marcus Whitman, a missionary who first made the Oregon trip in 1836, returned and led 1,000 settlers to Oregon with the help of John McLoughlin. For the following years accurate records are sketchy, but most historians agree that at least 350,000 emigrants had traveled the Oregon Trail by 1869.

The vast majority of travelers headed West chose the Oregon Trail for three main reasons: a fairly regular, good supply of water along the North Platte and Sweetwater Rivers; a dependable supply of grass across the prairie; and an easy, gradual grade to and through the mountains.

Originally called "The Emigrant Road" by the early pioneers, the route commonly became known as "The Oregon Trail" and later as "The Overland Trail". Regardless of its name, emigrants always referred to it as "the road" and not a "trail."❖

OREGON TRAIL HISTORY

LANDMARKS ALONG THE TRAIL

Landmarks offered many things to the pioneers. Not only were they used to mark time and gauge travel, but they also provided visual relief along often lonely and unexciting stretches of the trail.

Windlass Hill - Located at the entrance to Ash Hollow (found west of present-day Ogallala, Nebraska),this hill marked the most dangerous descent east of the Rockies. Wagons were windlassed down the hill; sometimes they broke loose from the ropes and careened to the floor of the hollow, 300 feet below, where they splintered on the rocks.

Chimney Rock is probably the most recognized natural feature along the Oregon Trail. It is made up of layers of Brule clay, volcanic ash and sandstone.

Ash Hollow - At the bottom of Windlass Hill, the pioneers discovered this valley of meadows and woods with a stream bubbling through it. This favorite camping place was often the first time the pioneers had seen shade since entering Nebraska. After camping a day or two, allowing the animals to rest and graze, the pioneers began the climb into the Rockies.

> **66 There were almost no trees for houses or fences and water was scarce except along the rivers. The land broiled in the summer and froze rock hard in the winter and the wind never seemed to blow itself out. 99**
>
> *~ Pioneer description of the Great American Desert*

Courthouse Rock - This natural Nebraska structure is situated about five miles south of the Platte River and reaches 400 feet into the air. Passing pioneers described it as looking like "the Capitol in Washington," "a cathedral in ruins," and "the Tower of Babel." Usually the wagon trains paused here so that the men and boys could take time to climb the fortress.

OREGON TRAIL HISTORY

Chimney Rock - Located in Nebraska 14 miles west of Courthouse Rock, this landmark is 500 feet tall, and the pioneers figured it took 10,040 steps to walk around its base. Chimney Rock has been said to look like a pole in a haystack, a church steeple, and an inverted funnel. Father DeSmet, a missionary passing by in 1840, was sure that in just a few years this structure would disintegrate into a heap of rocks on the prairie.

Scotts Bluff - A wagon train traveling on schedule would reach the bluff by late June. Located outside of Gering, Nebraska, it was named for Hiram Scott, a mountain man who died at its foot from illness. Two more days of travel would bring the pioneers to Fort Laramie.

Fort Laramie - This Wyoming fort served as the most important outpost along the trail. While camped here, pioneers spent their time writing letters home, washing clothes, mending wagons and harnesses, shoeing horses and oxen, and restocking supplies. Outside of Fort Laramie began the ascent into the Rockies, trying both the pioneers and the animals. Often the loads had to be lightened, which might mean leaving behind a sheet-iron stove, anvil, table or furniture.

Emigrant's Wash Tub - This hot spring, located southwest of Guernsey, Wyoming, was a welcome stop along the trail. The water stayed at 70° year-round, and the pioneer women used to stop and do their laundry here.

Three Island Crossing is near present-day Glenn's Ferry, Idaho. This site allowed the wagon trains to cross the treacherous Snake River by using three islands as stepping stones.

Register Cliff - At this popular pioneer camping place, about a day's travel west of Fort Laramie, emigrants took the time to leave a record of their progress. This sandstone cliff is covered with the names, hometowns, states and dates of pioneers who passed by on their way to Oregon.

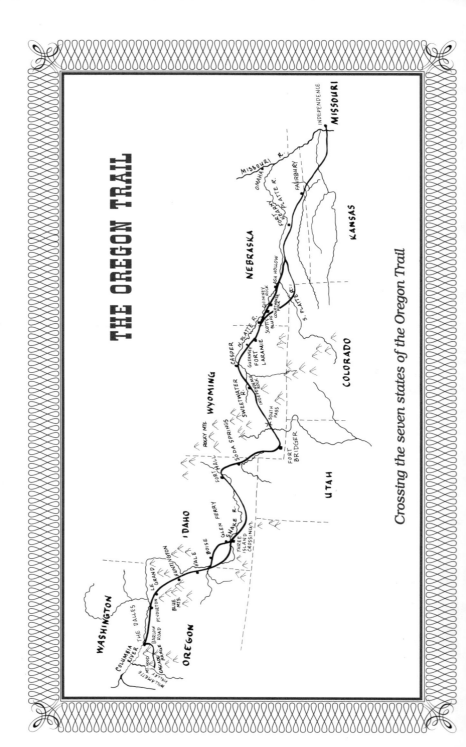

Crossing the seven states of the Oregon Trail

OREGON TRAIL HISTORY

Independence Rock - Named by the fur trappers who celebrated the Fourth of July there sometime between 1825 and 1830, this rock became the most anticipated of all Oregon Trail landmarks. Here the trail met the cool, clean Sweetwater River of Wyoming. Pioneers stopped to inscribe their names on the "Great Register of the Desert" and to rest themselves and their livestock while they observed Independence Day.

Pioneers crossing the Blue Mountains that border the Columbia River Valley in Oregon.

Devil's Gate - Found five miles from Independence Rock is a 400 foot deep chasm in a granite ridge. Too treacherous to traverse, many pioneers waded in the Sweetwater River through the gorge while the wagons followed the Oregon Trail through a pass to the east.

Split Rock - This dominant Wyoming landmark, the "gun sight" notch of Split Rock, aimed the emigrants directly at the South Pass, still more than 75 miles away.

South Pass - This windswept upland in the Wind River Mountains, west of present-day South Pass City, Wyoming, marked the halfway point of the trail. It sloped gradually over a broad grassy meadow, then dipped down toward the Pacific. Often the travelers were not sure they had crossed the Divide until they reached Pacific Springs a few miles down the trail.

Soda Springs - Just inside the Idaho border, these naturally carbonated waters would cause bread to rise. Some pioneers thought the water tasted like beer, others noted that it made good lemonade when mixed with citrus syrup and sugar.

Fort Hall - Fort Hall was located fifty-five miles past Soda Springs on the Snake River in southern Idaho. It was built in 1834 by Nat Wyeth as a trading post. A few miles past Fort Hall, the Oregon Trail split into two trails; one continuing to Oregon, the other to California. The next 300 miles of the Oregon Trail twisted along the Snake River's south rim to the Blue Mountains. Once over the mountains, the pioneers had to decide whether to float 230 miles down the treacherous Columbia or trek 250 miles over the Cascades to the Willamette Valley.

> **God never made a mountain that he did not make a place for some man to go over it or around it. I am going to hunt for that place.**
>
> ~ Samuel Barlow, 1845, Mount Hood

Barlow Road - In 1845, Samuel Barlow completed a wagon road over the mountains south of Mount Hood (Oregon) which became the standard emigrant route to western Oregon. Though safer than the river route, the Barlow Road plunged so steeply in places that settlers had to let their wagons down the sides using ropes wrapped around trees.

ARE WE THERE YET?

From Independence, Missouri to Oregon City in the Willamette Valley, the Oregon Trail ran 2,000 zig-zagging miles across the present states of Missouri, Kansas, Nebraska, Wyoming, Idaho, Washington and Oregon. The distance in miles mattered less than the distance in time. It usually took at least four and one-half months to reach the West, and the trip became a race against the seasons. Most wagon trains traveled at an average speed of 12 to 20 miles per day; but sometimes only a mile or two a day if climbing mountains.

Late April or early May was the best time to get a wagon train moving. The departure date had to be calculated carefully. If the train started too early in the spring, there would not be enough grass on the prairie to graze the livestock. The animals would then become sick, slowing up the wagon train and causing changes in the schedule that could bring serious trouble later. On the other

OREGON TRAIL HISTORY

OREGON TRAIL HISTORY

hand, a wagon train that started after other trains were already on the road found trampled grass and polluted water holes. Worse yet, a train that waited too long could get trapped in the mountains by an early winter blizzard.❖

THE PRAIRIE SCHOONER - HOME ON WHEELS

Most important to the pioneers were their wagons and animals. A family man usually opted for the wagon. Although it was the costliest and the slowest, it provided space and shelter for his children and wife. A new wagon cost anywhere from $60 to $90. It was usually 10' x 4' (about the size of a mini van) and did not hold more than the barest necessities. Seasoned travelers recommended that the wagons be made as simply as possible, using strong, light, well-seasoned lumber (maple, hickory or oak), and that the wheels be made of Osage orange wood.

The wheels were quite tall to clear prairie grass, rivers and rocks. However, this limited maneuverability because the wagons could not make sharp turns; tongues often snapped in half if the animals pulled too hard to either side. The wheels themselves often fell apart. The dry air of the plains resulted in shrinking the wooden spokes and rims, causing the iron tires to wobble off. Breakdowns had to be repaired quickly, and it was not unusual for a dining room table to become a new wheel.

The cover of the wagon was usually made of heavy cotton twill or canvas and waterproofed with linseed oil. Pockets and slings were often sewn to the inside for added storage. Supported by curved bows, there was about five feet of headroom in a wagon. Pucker ropes at either end could be tightened to screen out the sun, rain or dust.

Oxen were the most commonly used draft animals on the Oregon Trail. They could pull greater loads than mules and did not require a daily feeding of grain.

OREGON TRAIL HISTORY

Regarding the choice of animals, arguments could be made either way, for or against, oxen versus mules. Mules were more sure-footed, smart, quick moving and more durable during the summer heat, and cost $90 to $100 each. Oxen, however, could pull heavier loads, would eat anything, did not run away at night, were less likely to be stolen by Indians and did not cost as much ($50 per ox). Oxen were also patient, gentle and could be used for food, if necessary. On the down side, they were slow, plodding along rather than walking, and their hooves splintered on the mountain rocks and had to be wrapped in buffalo skin and rested until repaired.

A wagon traveling with oxen at the helm usually required about 15 more days of travel than one with mules. Generally, a minimum of two teams of mules or two yoke of oxen were required to pull a loaded wagon. Of course, the more teams the better, so that the animals did not have to work as hard, and if any died, the rest could still successfully pull the loaded wagon.❖

ONLY THE NECESSITIES

Before setting off from the chosen "jump off" point, the pioneers would purchase the provisions necessary for the trip. Once loaded, there was little space left for extras or riders. The inventory for provisions varied, but by and large included food, cooking utensils, clothing, tools, bedding, weapons and luxury items if there was extra space.

As a rule of thumb, the following food provisions would last an adult 110 days:

✓ 150 pounds of flour or its equivalent in hardtack
✓ 25 pounds of bacon or pork
✓ 25 pounds of fresh beef on the trail
✓ 20 pounds of beans
✓ 8 pounds of rice
✓ 30 - 40 pounds of dried fruit and vegetables
✓ 15 pounds of coffee (and tea)

✓ 25 - 40 pounds of sugar
✓ 5 pounds of baking soda
✓ 5 - 10 gallons of whiskey (for medicinal purposes)
✓ 1 cow for milk
✓ 1 jug molasses
✓ yeast powder for bread
✓ salt and pepper

OREGON TRAIL HISTORY

To keep bacon, it was packed in boxes or barrels and covered with bran, which prevented the fat from melting. Cured pork was also packed in this manner, but did not usually keep as long and had to be eaten up more quickly. Flour was packed in hundred pound sacks. To keep sugar from dissolving, it was packed in India-rubber sacks. Butter could be taken along by boiling it thoroughly and skimming off the scum as it rose to the top. It was then placed in canisters and soldered shut. This method of preservation kept it sweet for quite a long time. Eggs were packed in cornmeal, and as the eggs were used up, the cornmeal was used to make bread. Everyone drank coffee--adults, children and animals--when the water was not palatable to drink.

Pioneers could often count on killing a few buffalo or antelope along the way, but a more dependable source of fresh meat was a

herd of cattle driven behind the wagons. A milk cow also usually accompanied the pioneers. In case of a storm when it was impossible to cook, milk could substitute for a meal. Milk could also be churned into butter by hanging it in a pail beneath the jolting wagon. By the end of the day, the butter would be ready.❖

Buffalo were both valuable and a nuisance. Stampeding buffalo stopped at nothing and caused serious damage to wagon trains in their path.

WHAT'S COOKING?

Twice a day, in the morning and evening, pioneer cooks built cookfires and prepared their meals. Cooking conditions were primitive. Pioneer kitchens had the sky for a roof and prairie grass for the floor. Since there was little wood to be found, dried buffalo chips were gathered from the prairie and used to build fires. It is said the chips burned like peat and produced no unpleasant taste. Since the heat from such a fire was quite unreliable, a cook never knew if her bread would come out burnt on the bottom or uncooked in the middle.

Breakfast usually consisted of bread with fried pork, bacon or buffalo meat and coffee. The noonday meal had to be eaten quickly, and there usually was no time to build a fire. Typically the menu consisted of a sandwich and coffee. The evening meal was usually hot, though not elaborate, and varied from day to day by adding pickles, baked beans, biscuits, or as a special treat, dessert.

Stops for fully cooked, hot meals were rare. A meal normally consisted of bread or hardtack, salt pork and boiled coffee.

Yeast bread was made by the sponge method using a yeast starter. Pioneer women timed the rising and kneading of their bread dough so that it would be at just the right point for baking when the train stopped for the night.

Until the end of the 1800's, refined sugar was scarce and expensive. If it were available, it came in loaves or cubes. Brown sugar was more commonly used, as was molasses. The flour was unbleached and often had to be dried over the fire before using it. Coffee was sold green and had to be roasted and ground before brewing.

Cooking equipment was pared down to the essentials. Typically a pioneer woman's kitchen would include a Dutch oven, sheet-iron stove, skillet, kettle, coffee grinder, tin table service--coffee pot, tin cups, plates, silverware, butcher knife, ladle, large water keg and matches. Using these items, she was able to prepare a variety of stews, bake breads and pies, roast meat, or fry bacon or pork.

A kettle, one of the most necessary cooking utensils, could be used for several items at one time. Usually a stew would be bubbling

inside while bread was being steam baked above. Or, to speed the baking, the bread could be lowered into the stew in an enclosed tin container, to prevent liquid from leaking in, and thus steamed. In place of steaming bread in the kettle with the stew, a sweet pudding wrapped in a cloth bag might also be boiled at the same time.

The skillets used by pioneer women looked different than the ones we know today. Because there was no smooth surface to set the skillet on, it stood on three legs and became known as a spider.

Baking on the trail could be accomplished in a variety of ways. A sheet of tin arranged around the fire reflected the heat back onto the bread or pies, browning the top crusts while the fire baked the bottom. A better option was a portable metal box with an open side turned toward the fire and two or three shelves, so that several layers of bread, biscuits or pies could be baked at one time. When fitted with a domed top, which intensified the temperature inside, meat could be successfully roasted. If this option were not available, the meat was simply placed on the end of a long, sturdy fork and held over the coals.

One of the most useful cooking utensils was the Dutch oven. Virtually anything could be baked or roasted in this round, cast iron pot by placing the base on top of the hot coals and then placing more on the lid to provide heat from both the top and bottom. Its versatility allowed pioneer cooks to experiment with different recipes that would normally be baked in an oven.❖

LIFE GOES ON

> ❝ Made our beds down in the tent in the wet and mud. . .
> Cold and cloudy this morning and everybody out of
> humor. . . Have to eat cold supper. . . We are creeping
> along slowly. . . out of one mud hole and into another all
> day. ❞
>
> ~ Amelia Knight, 1853, on the Oregon Trail

Nothing could prepare the pioneers for the ordeals of the trail. They had imagined themselves building new homes and creating bright futures in the West, but the strain of getting there proved far worse than any guidebook had hinted at. Life on the trail was a story of an increasingly difficult roadway, of inadequate supplies of food and water, of draining weariness and miseries of every sort. Many lost sight of their original goal, but after a few weeks on the trail, most of them had come too far to return. Their only choice was to continue, not knowing what lay ahead.

Prairie storms often struck without warning, blackening the skies with dust whirling in 80 mile-an-hour winds. Canvas covers were ripped off by the wind and wheels bogged down in the mud. Rainstorms usually did not come as showers, but rather, downpours, which were accompanied by sharp, incessant flashes of lightning and continuous thunder. Many times after a rain, creeks and rivers rose and became impassable. Sometimes it took up to two weeks before they dropped enough to be crossed.

Sudden lightning storms left the traveling pioneers little time to circle up and corral their animals in an effort to prevent them from running blindly across the prairie.

Worse than a thunder storm, a prairie blizzard could devastate a wagon train overnight. As temperatures quickly dropped

OREGON TRAIL HISTORY

to -40°, cattle would inhale particles of sleet and snow which froze in their nostrils and caused them to die of suffocation.

Snow caused problems for the weary emigrants, too. When crossing the mountains, many pioneers suffered snow blindness. Caused by the reflection of sunlight off the gleaming white snow, a reliable method of prevention was to rub dampened black powder or charcoal under the eyes and across the nose.

In spite of all the the mishaps that took lives, both animal and human, disease was the greatest killer on the Oregon Trail. At least 20,000 emigrants--1 out of every 17 that started--were buried along the Oregon Trail; most succumbed to the very illnesses the pioneers were trying to escape. Fatalities on the trail were so numerous the emigrants averaged one grave every 80 yards between the Missouri River and the Willamette Valley.

"Died of cholera" was the most common epitaph along the trail. Only the higher elevation of the Rocky Mountains could prevent this disease. Death was so imminent for cholera victims that graves were often dug before the invalid had passed away. Burial services were stark and practical. Since there was not usually lumber available for coffins, the pioneers wrapped the bodies in cloths and buried them under rocks and packed earth or in the wagon ruts, in hopes that wolves or other wild animals would not paw them up.

The livestock, though necessary to complete the journey, also caused problems. At least two stops a day were required to rest and water the working animals. Grass and clean water were usually in good supply across Kansas and Nebraska, but rocky terrain and alkaline water ponds in the high plains took a heavy toll on the animals. If the food sources were not the cause of loss, many animals drowned crossing rivers, were run off by Indians, or scared into a frenzy by lightning storms. The loss of a mule or ox team could leave a wagon stranded.

OREGON TRAIL HISTORY

Except when traveling along the rivers, a sufficient supply of clean drinking water was always a problem. Fortunately, many pioneer women boiled their drinking water before making coffee or tea, so as to disguise its taste and help prevent infections.

Sometimes it was necessary when traveling along the Platte to sink a well in the quicksand. To do this, a flour barrel was perforated with small holes and forced into the sand. Then the undercurrent flowing through the sand would force the water into the barrel while the small holes kept most of the sand out. What did seep in acted as a filter and settled to the bottom of a pail if left overnight.

Although rainstorms were often violent, they also served as life savers when water was running low. A supply of drinking water could be obtained by catching the water as it dripped off a tent or by suspending a cloth or blanket by four corners and hanging a small weight in the center, so the water would run to one point. After the rain stopped, the cloth was drained into a barrel.

If by chance there were heavy dews in the morning, it was not unusual for the pioneers to collect water by spreading a blanket out on top of the grass. Then, with a stick or rope attached to one corner, it was dragged over the grass and wrung out as the water accumulated.❖

In spite of all the hardships endured, most of the physically and mentally exhausted travelers made it to the Columbia River Valley, finding that it was every bit as beautiful as they had heard. Emigrants soon became settlers and claimed the rewards of their paradise. They quickly settled and began building homes. Before long, the pioneers covered the 250,000 miles of land with wheat fields, dairy farms, sawmills and towns. They transformed the Pacific Northwest into the one of the richest and most bountiful regions of America. The luck and grit of these first pioneers had settled the West.❖

PRAIRIE RECIPES

*Cooking
on the
trail and
other old
favorites.*

WESTPORT LANDING

Pioneers came to Missouri, where civilization ended and the unknown began. Most people came from other nations and tamed lands further east. They arrived at Westport Landing in wagons, steamboats, on horseback and on foot.

Missouri was the "jumping off" or starting point for the Oregon Trail, as it was for all other trails heading west. Thus, Missouri became known as the "Gateway to the West". In the late 1840's and early 1850's, Westport Landing, now a suburb of Kansas City, became an important Oregon Trail departure point. The stores and businesses in Westport became prime suppliers to settlers heading west.

PRAIRIE RECIPES

Twice a day, for breakfast and supper, pioneer women built campfires of wood (when available), buffalo chips or sage brush and created basic, though nourishing, meals. Bread, bacon, salt-pork and coffee were the mainstays of their diet, supplemented by whatever fresh meat they encountered--buffalo, antelope, rabbit or prairie chicken. Dried fruits and vegetables were wisely prepared before beginning their journey.

Numerous things could go wrong at a campfire, and many meals were unintentionally garnished with blowing sand or ashes. No doubt rainstorms dampened more than one prairie picnic. In spite of nature's interference, they managed quite well, maintaining as much likeness to "home" as possible.

The recipes in this section have been collected from a variety of sources. Some are fairly close indicators of foods the pioneer women may have fixed, while others are updated versions.❖

PRAIRIE RECIPES

OLD TIMERS' HINTS AND HELPS

Weights of Groceries: Ten common sized eggs weigh one pound; soft butter the size of an egg weighs one ounce; one quart of sifted flour (well heaped) weighs one pound; one pint of best brown sugar weighs 13 ounces; two teacups (well heaped) of A sugar weighs one pound; two teacups (level) of granulated sugar weighs one pound; two teacups of soft butter (well packed) weighs one pound; one and one third pints of powdered sugar weighs one pound; two tablespoons of granulated sugar or flour weighs one ounce; 1 tablespoon (well rounded) of soft butter weighs one ounce; one pint (heaped) of granulated sugar, 14 ounces; one pound coffee A sugar weighs 12 ounces.

Weights and Measures: Two and a half teaspoonfuls makes one tablespoonful; four tablespoonfuls make one wineglassful; two wineglassfuls make one gill; two gills make one teacupful; two teacupfuls make one pint; four teaspoonfuls salt make one ounce; one and a half tablespoonfuls granulated sugar make one ounce; two tablespoonfuls flour make one ounce; one pint loaf sugar weighs 10 ounces; one pint brown sugar weighs 12 ounces; one pint granulated sugar weighs 16 ounces; one pint wheat flour weighs nine ounces; one pint cornmeal, 11 ounces; 10 ordinary sized eggs, about 16 ounces; a piece of butter the size of an egg, about one and a half ounces.

PRAIRIE RECIPES

CAMP FIRE BOILED BEANS

2 lbs. beans
1 T. baking soda
Water to cover
Diced bacon, ham or hocks

Soak 2 pounds of (white) Great Northern or Navy beans, making sure there is at least 1 1/2 inches or more of water over the beans; let soak overnight. In the morning, place on stove, making sure there is enough water to cover the beans. Let come to a boil, reduce heat and simmer 1/2 hour. Add 1 tablespoon baking soda, stir briskly, drain and rinse with cold water. Return to kettle, cover with water (1 1/2 inch) as before and place on stove, adding any of the following: diced bacon ends, ham (cut in 1/2-inch cubes), or ham ends or hocks. Ham bones can also be used. After bringing to a boil, reduce heat and let cook slowly for 3 hours or more, making sure they are covered with water.

BOSTON BAKED BEANS

Wash the required amount of beans, cover with cold water and place on the back of the stove until the water becomes tepid, then add a small piece of baking soda and bring it to a boil. Drain and cover again with boiling water, letting them simmer until the skins burst. Then take a genuine bean pot; put in half the beans, next a nice piece of salt pork (about half a pound to a pint of beans) and then the remaining beans with the liquor. Season with pepper; add a lump of butter. Cover closely and bake at an even temperature for five hours. Keep them covered with water for three hours, afterward allowing it to boil down. These may be baked in the afternoon and remain in the oven all night, to reheat for breakfast.

I was possessed with a spirit of adventure and a desire to see what was new and strange.
- Miriam A. Thompson, 1845

PRAIRIE RECIPES

EMIGRANT TURNIPS & RUTABAGAS

Peel the desired amount of turnips or rutabagas. Cut into pieces same as you would potatoes. Place in kettle; wash and drain. Cover with water. Let cook 35-40 minutes or until done. Mash, if desired, adding a little salt and pepper and enough milk and butter to make like mashed potatoes.

BUCK SKIN HASH

Chop a couple of small onions and put with a little water into a skillet or small kettle; cook until tender and nearly dry. Add a cupful of chopped meat and a little more than a cupful of mashed or chopped cold potatoes. Put in a good piece of butter and salt and pepper to taste. Stir all together, heat hot and serve at once.

PRAIRIE RECIPES

JOURNEYMAN'S CHICKEN PIE

An old chicken will do for this purpose, in fact, it is preferable to a very young one. Singe and draw the fowl, cutting it up in joints. Cover with cold water and let it simmer, closely covered, for an hour or more, according to its age. Then add three sliced medium-sized onions, some sprigs of parsley, and salt and pepper and continue the cooking until the meat is tender and the onions done. Dish the bulky pieces, such as the back, under part of the breast and first joints. Make a batter with one egg, a cup of milk and a teaspoonful of sea foam or baking powder sifted through enough flour to make it of cupcake consistency. Drop this into the boiling broth in small spoonfuls. While the dumplings are cooking, which will take about eight minutes, heat to boiling half a pint of milk; pour this into the gravy after the rest of the meat and the dumplings have been removed and stir in a lump of butter and a large tablespoonful of flour wet with a little cold milk; boil for a minute and pour over the chicken. The dumplings should be served on a separate dish. Bake a piece of rich pie crust the size of a dinner plate; break into as many pieces as there are people to be served and place as a border around the dish containing the meat. This is chicken pie par excellence and if your family is large, you need not be afraid to prepare two chickens. If any is left, heat for breakfast; add a little soup stock or thickened hot milk, if more gravy is necessary, and pour the whole over some slices of buttered toast. If the fowl is old and fat, it would be advisable to remove as much as possible of the fat and skin before cooking.

PRAIRIE RECIPES

SCRAPPLE

1 1/2 c. meat or more (pork)
1/2 c. onion
Cornmeal
1/2 c. celery
Sage (opt.)
Garlic (opt.)

Precook 6-8 fresh pork hocks or a pork neck bone in 5-6 cups of water, or more, until the meat can be removed from the bone. Meat may then be ground with a meat grinder and returned to the broth, adding the onion and celery. The sage and garlic may be added to taste. Let simmer until the onion and celery are cooked. Stir while cooking. Measure the liquid, adding 1 cup of cornmeal to 1 cup of cold water for every 3 cups of broth and meat. Let cook 5 minutes at low heat. When cooked, it may be put in a one-loaf bread pan. Let cool overnight in a cool place or in the refrigerator. May be sliced in slices 1/4-1/2 inch thick; fried on a hot griddle. Serve with butter, honey or syrup. **Note:** Measure liquid before adding meat.

HIGH NOON FRIED CHICKEN

Wash and cut up the chicken; wipe it dry. Season with salt and pepper; dredge it with flour or dip each piece in beaten egg and then in cracker crumbs. Have the lard hot in the frying pan and lay in the chicken. When brown on both sides, take up, drain and set aside in a covered dish. Stir into the gravy left, a large table-spoonful of flour; make it smooth. Add a cup of cream or milk; season with salt and pepper. Boil up and pour over the chicken. If the chicken is old, put into a stew pan with a little water and simmer gently until tender. Season with salt and pepper; dip in flour or cracker crumbs and egg and fry as above. Use the broth the chicken was cooked in to make the gravy instead of cream or milk, or use an equal quantity of both.

PRAIRIE RECIPES

STUFFING FOR GOOSE OR PIG

Sprinkle 1/2 cup sugar on 6 chopped apples, 1 cup stewed raisins and juice, 1 loaf of bread crumbs, salt, 2 eggs, butter or goose grease, cinnamon and cloves to taste; mix well. Stuff goose or pig.

GUN POWDER JERKY

Cut bison or venison in foot-long strips with the grain so it will be stringy, using any cut you can get strips from (rump, legs, etc.). Prepare a very strong salt and water brine and dip the strips in it until the meat is white. Hang strips in the sun until thoroughly dry and store in a ventilated container so that air can get to them. May be eaten dry or rehydrated. When stewed, jerky is very similar to fresh meat.

PAWNEE PEMMICAN

Combine equal parts of buffalo suet, dried fruit such as cherries, berries and plums and dried venison or other game. Add salt, if available, and pound the mixture in a bowl or a hollow rock; then form into bricks. Dry in the sun or near the fire in rainy weather. Pemmican may be eaten as is by biting off chunks, or bricks may be simmered in water to make a thick soup or stew.

PREPARING PEMMICAN

The buffalo meat is cut into thin flakes and hung up to dry in the sun or before a slow fire. It is then pounded between two stones and reduced to a powder. This powder is placed in a bag of the animal's hide with the hair on the outside. Melted grease is then poured into it and the bag sewn up.

PRAIRIE RECIPES

BASIC STARTER WITHOUT YEAST

1 c. flour
1/4 c. sugar
1 c. milk

Mix all ingredients together. Place in a loosely-covered container until the mixture doubles in size. This may take 4-14 days. When double, the starter is ready to use. Feed once or twice a week with 1 cup milk, 1 cup flour and 1/4 cup sugar.

SOURDOUGH GRIDDLE CAKES

2 c. sourdough starter
4 c. warm water
4 T. oil
1 tsp. salt
4 T. sugar
5 c. flour
2 eggs
1/2 c. condensed milk
2 tsp. baking soda

Mix starter, flour and warm water the night before. Reserve 2-3 cups to replenish starter. To what is left, add eggs, oil and milk; mix well. In a separate bowl, add sugar, salt and soda. Sprinkle over dough and gently fold in. Let rise 3-4 minutes. Fry on hot griddle. Serve immediately.

PRAIRIE RECIPES

SANDHILLS SOURDOUGH BREAD

2 c. starter
3/4 tsp. baking soda
1 T. shortening
1 c. flour or enough to make a kneadable dough

When all ingredients are mixed together with enough flour, it should form a kneadable dough. Then shape into a loaf and place into a greased bread pan. After being left in a warm place for a time, 1/2-1 hour, it should rise to about twice its size. Bake in a moderate oven for about an hour.

FLAT LAND SALT-RISING BREAD

Take about half a gallon of warm water; add to it salt, soda and sugar, of each a lump about as large as an ordinary pea. A spoonful of cornmeal improves it, though not necessary; stir in flour to the consistency of thick batter. A vessel holding about a gallon should be placed in a larger vessel and surrounded by warm water and kept warm for four or five hours, when it will have become light, perhaps filling the vessel. If while it was kept warm in a place there should be any water rise on it, pour it off. Now that it is light, get your flour into the kneading pan. Take about a pint of scalding water and scald part of the flour; then add enough cold water to cool the scalded flour. Now add your rising and knead until smooth, but do not make it so stiff as for hop yeast bread. When the dough has become smooth, mold and put it in your baking pans and keep in a warm place to rise. When ready to bake, it will require a hotter fire than for yeast bread. When baked, wrap in a wet cloth and set away to cool.

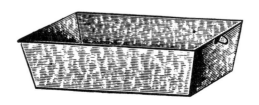

PRAIRIE RECIPES

JOHNNY CAKES

3 handfuls white cornmeal
1 handful flour
Pinch of salt
Boiling water to make smooth batter

Bake on hot, greased iron skillet until nicely browned on each side.

CHIMNEY ROCK CAKE

$^1/_2$ c. lard
$^1/_3$ c. sugar
3 eggs, beaten together
1 c. sweet milk
1 $^1/_2$ c. flour
1 $^1/_2$ c. cornmeal
1 tsp. baking powder
1 T. salt

Mix and drop on greased pan, 2 spoonfuls in a place and bake at 350° until golden brown.

COLD FLOUR

Cold Flour is made by parching corn and pounding it in a mortar to the consistency of coarse meal; a little sugar and cinnamon added makes it quite palatable. When the traveler becomes hungry or thirsty, a little of the flour is mixed with water and drunk. It is an excellent article for a traveler who desires to go the greatest length of time upon the smallest amount of transportation. It is said that half a bushel is sufficient to subsist a man for thirty days.

PRAIRIE RECIPES

CIRCLING-UP DOUGHNUTS

Three eggs, two cupfuls of sugar, one and one-half cupfuls of milk, butter the size of a small egg, two teaspoonfuls cream of tartar rubbed into a quart of flour, one teaspoonful soda dissolved in milk, a little salt and one half nutmeg. Use flour enough to roll out soft; cut in fancy shapes and drop into boiling lard. A slice of raw potato put in the fat will prevent it from burning.

CASCADE CRACKERS

To make good and healthful crackers, take, for five cups of good flour, one cup of melted butter; rub it well into the flour; then put one teaspoonful of soda in a bowl and pour a little warm water on it and dissolve. Have ready two teaspoonfuls of cream of tartar and put a cupful of cold water into the bowl that has the soda in it. When ready to turn into the flour, add the cream of tartar and pour in while it is effervescing. Mix your dough and roll out half as thick as a cracker ought to be and cut in squares or small rounds. Bake in a well heated oven.

WOODEN SPOON BREAD

2 c. white flour
1 T. baking powder
1 T. sugar
$1/2$ tsp. salt
1 c. milk
1 egg, beaten
$1/4$ c. lard

Sour milk may be used instead of the sweet, but stir in $1/2$ teaspoon soda if you use it. Sift dry ingredients; add milk and mix. Beat in egg; add melted lard and stir well. Drop from tablespoon into large baking pan. Bake 20 minutes in a quick oven.

PRAIRIE RECIPES

SADDLE SODA BISCUITS

Take four large cups of sifted flour, in which one large teaspoon soda and two teaspoons cream of tartar have been well mixed, with one teaspoon salt; add one half cup butter and a mix thoroughly. To this, add a pint of sweet milk, a little at a time, and mix with as little kneading as possible. Bake quickly.

MITCHELL PASS MUSH

No one ever "took sick" from eating mush and milk or fried mush in any suitable quantity. "Mush and milk" is seldom relished because few people know how to make the mush. The whole secret is in cooking it thoroughly. Rightly made it is not "hasty pudding." A well made "mush" is one that has boiled not less than a full hour. Two hours are better. The meal needs to be cooked; then it is both good and palatable. The rule is: mix it very thin and boil it down, avoiding any burning or scorching, and salt it just right to suit the general taste. Prepare a good kettle full for supper, to be eaten with milk, sugar, molasses, syrup or sweetened cream or sweetened milk. If a good supply be left to cook, and be cut in slices and fried well in the morning, the plate of wheaten bread will be little in demand. It must be fried well, not crisped or burned or soaked in fat. If thoroughly soaked through in the kettle, it will only need to be heated through on the griddle. If not cooked well in the kettle, longer frying will be necessary.

GOOD YEAST

Boil one pound good flour, a quarter of a pound of moist (lump or New Orleans) sugar and half an ounce of salt in two gallons of water for an hour. When nearly cold, bottle and cork it closely. It will be fit for use in twenty-four hours and one pint will make eighteen pounds of bread.

In. . . this journey, the emigrant should never forget that it is one in which time is everything.
- 1849 guidebook

PRAIRIE RECIPES

PLAINS BUCKWHEAT CAKES

Mix one gill of wheat flour with one quart of buckwheat flour and one large tablespoonful of salt, then add gradually a scant quart of warm water mixed with one gill of yeast. Let it rise all night and in the morning add a quarter of a teaspoonful of carbonate of soda and bake immediately on a smooth, well greased iron griddle, taking care to scrape it well after each baking and using as little grease as possible. The cakes should not be larger than a small saucer and should be served at once.

OLD FASHIONED GRAHAM BREAD

Prepare a sponge as for white bread; put into your baking pan the next morning a proportionate quantity of flour, two thirds graham and one third white, to every quart of which you will allow a large handful of Indian meal and a teaspoonful of salt. Make a hole in the center of this and pour in your sponge with two tablespoonfuls of molasses for each medium-sized loaf. The dough must be very soft. It will take a longer time to rise than white bread; when light, knead again, make into loaves and set in a warm place for a second raising. Bake steadily in a moderate oven for a much longer time then you would allow for white bread. Rapid baking will spoil it. In this, as in most housekeeping duties, you must acquire judgement by experience. The most essential point in the making of the dough is to keep it very soft.

PRAIRIE RECIPES

HARDTACK

1 cake yeast
1/2 c. warm water
1 lg. potato
2 c. potato water
4 c. graham flour
3 T. syrup
1 T. salt
1 c. bacon fat or other shortening
3 c. white flour

Dissolve yeast in warm water. Boil and mash potato. Cool potato water to lukewarm and make a sponge of yeast and potato, adding 2 cups graham flour. Let rise until foamy and bubbly. Add syrup, salt, shortening, 2 cups graham flour and about 3 cups white flour or enough to make a stiff dough. Let rise once to double in bulk and roll out very thin, placing on flat baking dish. Let rise and prick with fork. Bake until crisp.

SUNRISE SPONGE CAKE

Take four eggs, two coffee cups of sugar, two coffee cups of flour, two teaspoons of cream of tartar, one teaspoon of soda, two thirds of a cup of boiling water and lemon to flavor. Beat egg yolks and sugar well together; add the egg whites, whisked to a froth, alternately with the flour through which the soda and cream of tartar are sifted. Add the water and flavoring last. Bake in shallow tin in a well heated oven. This, though apparently thin, will be a delightful cake.

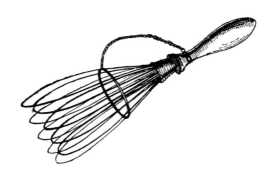

PRAIRIE RECIPES

VINEGAR DIP

2 c. water
1 1/2 c. sugar
2 heaping T. flour
2 T. vinegar or more
1/2 tsp. lemon extract

Bring water and sugar to a boil. Mix flour with enough water to make a medium paste. Add to above syrup. Add vinegar and lemon extract. This may be poured on pieces of spice cake.

PIONEER LEMON PIE

2 eggs
1 1/2 c. sugar
1/4 c. vinegar
2 c. water
7 level T. flour or more, if needed
1/2 tsp. lemon extract
1 T. butter

Add all ingredients in kettle and beat well. Cook at a low heat or in a double boiler until it thickens. Add 1 tablespoon butter and 1/2 teaspoon lemon extract and mix well. Pour into baked pie shell. Top with meringue or whipped cream. **Note:** This pie was made in earlier days when fresh lemons were not always on hand, so they would substitute vinegar and lemon extract for lemon juice.

SUN DRIED APPLE PIE

Wash the fruit thoroughly; soak overnight in water enough to cover. In the morning, stew slowly, until nearly done, in the same water. Sweeten to taste. The crust, both upper and under, should be rolled thin; a thick crust to a fruit pie is undesirable.

PRAIRIE RECIPES

TO MAKE A CAKE WITHOUT BUTTER

Take a piece of salt pork and melt it down and strain it through a piece of muslin. Set it aside until cool. It is then white and firm and may be used like butter in any kind of cake.

TO MAKE SUGAR OF SORGHUM

Boil sorghum thick, draw off in open coolers and place in a warm room. In about ten days it will be sufficiently granulated. Then place it into barrels or funnel shaped boxes with perforated bottoms and allow it to stand in a warm room to drain off the molasses and in a short time you will have sugar for use.

EGGLESS, MILKLESS, BUTTERLESS CAKE

1 c. brown sugar
1/3 c. lard
1 c. raisins
1 tsp. nutmeg
1 tsp. cinnamon
1/2 tsp. salt
2 c. flour
4 tsp. baking powder
3/4 c. chopped nuts
1 1/4 c. water

Boil sugar, water, raisins, lard, salt and spices for 3 minutes. When cooked, add flour and baking powder and mix well. Bake in a one loaf bread pan in a moderate oven for 45 minutes.

PRAIRIE RECIPES

SUET PUDDING

3 c. flour
2 tsp. baking powder
1 tsp. salt
1 tsp. cinnamon
1 tsp. nutmeg
$1/2$ tsp. cloves
1 c. seeded raisins
$1/2$ c. walnuts
1 c. ground suet
1 c. unsulfured molasses
1 c. milk

Sift dry ingredients in one bowl. Put suet through food chopper. Add unsulfured molasses and milk. Combine wet and dry ingredients. Stir in raisins and walnuts. Fill greased pudding mold $3/4$ full; cover tightly. Steam for about 3 $1/2$ hours. Serve warm with Hard Sauce.

WILD GOOSEBERRY COBBLER

1 c. sugar
1 c. flour
2 T. butter
2 c. gooseberries
$3/4$ c. milk
2 tsp. baking powder
$1/8$ tsp. salt
1 more c. sugar

Cream sugar, flour and butter; add milk, baking powder and salt. Mix. Pour batter in 8 x 8-inch baking dish. On top of batter, spread gooseberries (or any other fruit) over which sprinkle 1 cup sugar. Add 1 cup (or less) hot water over all. Bake in moderate oven for 30 minutes.

PRAIRIE RECIPES

SODA SPRINGS LEMONADE

Upon the very thin rind and juice of four good sized lemons, put sugar to your taste and three pints of boiling water. The lemonade should be made thirty-six or forty-eight hours before using it. Leave the peel in one day. Strain before using.

CLEARWATER GINGER BEER

One pound of loaf sugar, one ounce of cream of tartar, one and a half ounces of best white ginger (bruised), one gallon of boiling water. Pour the water upon these ingredients and let it stand until the next morning when it may be bottled. It is better to strain it through muslin when bottled.

A GOOD RECEIPT FOR VINEGAR

Take forty gallons of water, one gallon of molasses and four pounds of acetic acid. It will be fit for use in a few days. This is the receipt by which most of the cider vinegar is made which is sold in the country stores.

WASHINGTON APPLE BEER

Peel your apples and dry the peelings in the sun or by the stove. Put them in a crock and add enough boiling water to cover them. Cover the crock and let it sit for one or two days until all the flavor comes out of the peelings. You may add some sugar, if you want.

PRAIRIE RECIPES

TIN CUP COFFEE
(In Large Quantity)

For an ordinary wash boiler, use three pounds of coffee; divide into two parts. To each part, add two eggs and enough cold water to wet it thoroughly; put half of this into each of two 12 x 8-inch bags (cheesecloth). Let the water be hot, but not boiling, when coffee is put into it. When comes to a boil, your coffee will be excellent.

FRESH CREAM BUTTER

Partially fill a butter churn with thick cream. Operate the churn until the fat separates from the fluid milk. Remove the butter from the churn or jar. Add a small amount of salt. Shape the butter by pressing into a small bowl or butter press. Sometimes churn was fastened to the covered wagon and the "bouncing" of the wagon all day long produced butter for the evening meal.

COOKING BUTTER

One pound kidney suet cut in small pieces and melted over a slow fire; add one pound butter. Melt and strain through a sieve.

VANILLA EXTRACT

To one vanilla bean cut in small pieces, add half a pint of alcohol and let stand for several weeks before using.

LEMON EXTRACT

Pare a lemon, being careful to use only the outside yellow. Put in a jar and cover with alcohol and let stand for several weeks before using.

PRAIRIE RECIPES

BAKING POWDER

One pound pure cream of tartar, half pound common baking soda, quarter of a pound cornstarch; sift six or seven times together. Put away in an airtight jar; ready for use at once.

ARROWROOT

Use milk or water as preferred; put a heaping teaspoonful ground arrowroot into a cup and mix with a little cold milk. Stir into a pan containing a pint of either cream or water that has been brought to a boil, adding a little salt. Let it simmer a few minutes and then pour out. May be sweetened or flavored with grated nutmeg as desired; should be made only as it is wanted.

BAKED MILK

Put the milk in a jar, covering the opening with white paper, and bake in a moderate oven until thick as cream. May be taken by the most delicate stomach.

A DAINTY SOUP

Boil a small chicken in enough water to cover it; skim and strain when done. Make a mustard of one well beaten egg, a little salt, half a pint of milk; put it in a cup and set in boiling water until it is done. Then with a teaspoon, cut out dumplings and drop them into your soup.

PANADA

Put two or three soda crackers into a bowl; pour boiling water over them until they are swelled. Sprinkle a little sugar over them; add a cup of boiling water and a tablespoonful of wine and flavor to taste.

PRAIRIE RECIPES

WINE POSSET

In one pint of milk, boil two or three slices of bread; when soft, remove from the stove. Add a little nutmeg and one teaspoon sugar and then pour into it slowly one-half pint sweet wine. Serve it with toasted bread.

WINE WHEY

One pint sweet milk; boil and pour into it sherry wine until it curdles, then strain and use whey.

SEVEN STATE RECIPES

The following recipes come from the seven states that the pioneers traveled across.

MISSOURI BAKED CHICKEN AND GRAVY

3-3 $^1/_2$ lbs. chicken
$^1/_4$ c. flour
$^1/_4$ c. melted butter
$^2/_3$ c. evaporated milk
1 can cream of mushroom soup
1 c. shredded Velveeta cheese
$^1/_2$ tsp. salt
$^1/_8$ tsp. pepper
$^1/_4$ lb. fresh mushrooms, sliced
Onion powder to taste
Dash of paprika

Coat chicken with flour. Bake, uncovered, in melted butter with chicken skin side down for 30 minutes at 425°. Turn chicken and bake for 15-20 more minutes or until tender. Pour off excess fat from chicken. Combine soup, cheese, salt and pepper. Spoon onto chicken. Top with mushrooms. Pour evaporated milk on top. Sprinkle with paprika. Cover with foil. Bake at 325° for 20-30 minutes.

PRAIRIE RECIPES

SHOW-ME STATE PUDDING

1 egg
3/4 c. sugar
2 heaping T. flour
1 1/4 tsp. baking powder
1/8 tsp. salt
1 tsp. vanilla
1/2 c. chopped nuts
1 c. raw, chopped apples

Beat egg and sugar until smooth. Add salt and vanilla. Sift in flour and baking powder. Add nuts and apples. Pour in greased pie pan and bake at 350° for 35 minutes.

KANSAS CITY STUFFED PORK CHOPS

4 chops, cut about 1 1/2 inch thick with pocket slit in middle

Stuff with cornbread dressing and bake in cooking bag at least 45 minutes to an hour. **Cornbread Dressing:** Make cornbread. Add dried bread crumbs, about 3/4 package. Season to taste with salt, pepper and sage. Saute 3/4 cup onions and finely chopped celery in 1 stick oleo. Moisten with 1 egg and chicken broth. Stuff chops and bake. Leftover dressing can be cooked and served on side as you can't put too much dressing in chops.

PRAIRIE RECIPES

SUNFLOWER DIRT CAKE

1 lg. pkg. Oreo cookies
1 (8-oz.) pkg. cream cheese
1/2 c. butter or margarine
1 c. powdered sugar
1 lg. ctn. Cool Whip
2 (3.4-oz.) pkgs. instant vanilla pudding
3 c. milk
1 tsp. vanilla

Crush cookies and put 1/2 cookie crumbs in 9 x 13-inch pan. Mix cream cheese and butter until smooth. Mix in powdered sugar. Fold in Cool Whip. In a separate bowl, mix milk, pudding and vanilla. Fold the 2 mixtures together and pour into the pan over the crumbs. Spread remaining crumbs over top. Can be served frozen or chilled.

CORNHUSKER BAKED BEEF BRISKET

5 lbs. beef brisket
1/2 c. vinegar
1 1/2 c. water
1 stick butter
Dash of salt & pepper
1 c. water
1 stick butter

Barbecue Sauce:

1/2 c. brown sugar
2 c. ketchup
2 T. Worcestershire sauce
2 T. cooking sherry
Butter

Warm first five ingredients and pour over meat. Soak overnight. Pour off liquid. Add the 1 cup water and 1 stick butter. Bake at 250° for 5 1/2 hours. Cook thoroughly, then slice. Pour barbecue sauce on top and place in refrigerator until ready to serve. Warm slowly in oven before serving at low heat.

PRAIRIE RECIPES

NEBRASKA FRESH CORN ON THE COB
(Microwave)

Choose the freshest corn available and of uniform size. If the husks seem dry, rinse the ears briefly in cool water; then lay them, no more than four ears at a time, one inch apart on the microwave oven floor. An extra two ears can go on the shelf above, but no more as the corn won't cook evenly. Microwave, uncovered, on high, using the following as a guide: 1 ear for 2 to 3 minutes; 2 ears for 3 to 4 minutes; 4 ears for 5 to 6 minutes; 6 ears for 7 to 8 minutes. At half time, turn ears over and rearrange, moving those on outside toward center and vice versa. Check for doneness after minimum cooking time by peeling husks back slightly and pressing a few kernels; they should feel springy-firm. Remove ears from microwave and let stand, in husk, 3 minutes. Let everyone shuck his own corn. The silks magically come away with the husks and the corn's flavors are all the better for being steamed in its natural wrapper. Pass the melted butter or butter sauce.

COWBOY ROAST LEG OF LAMB

1 leg of lamb
1/2 c. Dijon mustard
3 T. soy sauce
2 garlic cloves, crushed
1 tsp. dried rosemary
1/2 tsp. marjoram
1/2 tsp. thyme
Fresh lemon juice

Preheat oven to 350°. Combine the mustard, soy sauce, garlic, rosemary, thyme, marjoram and lemon juice in a bowl; blend well. Brush the lamb with the mustard sauce. Lower heat to 325°; continue roasting until meat thermometer registers desired degree of doneness.

PRAIRIE RECIPES

WYOMING PEACH COBBLER

1 1/2 lbs. (3 c.) fresh peaches
3/4 c. sugar
1/4 tsp. mace
1 c. all-purpose flour
1 tsp. baking powder
3/4 c. milk
2 lg. eggs, lightly beaten
6 T. butter

Heat oven to 375°. In medium bowl, toss peaches, 1/4 cup sugar and mace to mix well. In second bowl, combine flour, remaining sugar and baking powder. Stir in milk and eggs until just blended. Place butter in 9-inch square baking pan; set in oven until butter is melted and hot. Immediately pour batter over butter; spoon peach mixture evenly over batter. Bake 40-45 minutes until puffed and brown.

IDAHO SALMON POTATO STRATA

6 potatoes, unpared, sliced
1 (16-oz.) can salmon
1 whole lemon
1/2 c. celery, stringed, chopped
1/2 c. onions, chopped green/yellow
2 c. lowfat milk
1/8 tsp. pepper
4 eggs
1/4 tsp. dill weed
1 1/2 tsp. salt, divided
Paprika/Parmesan to taste
1/4 tsp. garlic salt or fresh minced garlic

Combine salmon, onion, celery, eggs, milk, half of salt, dill, garlic salt and pepper in a large bowl; mix well. Layer half of potatoes (sliced thin) in a 1 1/2-quart baking dish. Sprinkle with 1/2 teaspoon salt and spread 1/2 of salmon mixture over potatoes. Repeat same with remaining mixture. Bake at 350° for 75 minutes, uncovered. Sprinkle with paprika and Parmesan as desired. Garnish with celery tops and thin slices of twisted fresh lemon.

PRAIRIE RECIPES

BOISE POTATO BREAD

2 pkgs. yeast dissolved in 1/2 c. warm water
2 tsp. salt
6 c. white flour
1 c. whole-wheat flour, unsifted
2 c. potato water
1/2 c. honey
2 eggs, beaten
1/2 stick margarine
1/4 c. oil

Heat potato water, honey, margarine and oil together until margarine is melted; cool. Add eggs, yeast mixture and 2 cups flour, salt and beat. Stir in enough extra flour (about 4 1/2 cups) to form a soft dough. Knead with the remaining flour for about 5 minutes. Cover and sit in a warm spot. Let dough rise to double, punch down and let rise again. Divide dough into 2 loaves. Let rise until double and bake in 350° oven for 45 minutes.

PACIFIC OYSTER ROAST

1 qt. Pacific oysters
1 clove garlic, minced
1/2 c. olive oil
3/4 c. Parmesan cheese
1/2 c. cracker meal
1/2 tsp. salt
1/4 tsp. pepper

Preheat the oven to 450°. Mix the cracker meal and cheese together. Mix the oil and garlic together. Dip each oyster in the garlic/oil mixture and then in the cheese/cracker meal mixed with the salt and pepper. Place in a greased baking dish or divide into small, greased ramekins. Bake for 30 minutes. **Very rich!**

PRAIRIE RECIPES

FRESH WASHINGTON BLACKBERRY PIE

5 c. blackberries
2 1/2 c. flour
1 1/4 c. plus 1 T. sugar
1/2 tsp. vanilla
1/2 tsp. almond extract
2 tsp. lemon juice
2/3 c. plus 2 T. shortening
1/3 c. milk
1 T. butter
Salt

Toss blackberries, 1/2 cup flour, 1 1/4 cups sugar, 1/8 teaspoon salt, vanilla, almond extract and lemon juice until well mixed. Set aside. Sift flour, salt and sugar. Cut in shortening. Pour in milk. Mix pastry and roll. Fill pie shell with blackberries. Dot with butter. Cover with top crust. Bake at 425°.

OREGON SALMON

6 salmon steaks, 3/4 inch thick
1 T. lemon juice
Salt & pepper
2 egg whites
3/4 c. mayonnaise
1/2 c. cheddar cheese (2 oz.), finely shredded
1/4 c. chopped green onion
2 T. finely chopped fresh parsley
1 tsp. dill weed
Pinch of red (cayenne) pepper

Preheat broiler. Generously grease a broiling pan. Arrange salmon steak on greased pan. Sprinkle with lemon juice. Season lightly with salt and pepper. Broil 4-6 inches from heat, 6-8 minutes or until fish tests done. Meanwhile, in a bowl, beat egg whites until stiff but not dry. Fold in mayonnaise, cheese, onions, parsley, dill, pinch of salt and pepper. Spread mixture evenly over fish; broil until lightly browned. Makes 6 servings.

PRAIRIE RECIPES

NORTHERN APPLE PIE WITH CRUMB TOPPING

Topping: (combine)

1/2 c. sugar
3/4 c. flour
1/3 c. butter or oleo

Cut together like pie crust. Sprinkle over apples in pie shell.

Apple Pie:

4 c. sliced apples
3/4-1 c. sugar
1/8 tsp. salt
1 tsp. cinnamon
2 T. flour

Toss together so apples are coated. Put apples in crust and put topping over apples. Bake at 450° for 10 minutes. Reduce heat to 350° for 40 minutes.

Recipe Favorites

WILD GAME RECIPES

Rabbit,
buffalo,
antelope,
deer,
bear,
or my cow.

OLD FORT KEARNY

Fort Kearny was one of the most important posts on the Oregon Trail. It was established in 1848 in central Nebraska near present day Kearney, and sits along the south bank of the Platte River. Travelers stopped at its adobe storehouses to make repairs and buy supplies that the commanding officer was authorized to sell to them at cost. If the families were in want, the soldiers often gave them provisions free of charge. Fort Kearny was never attacked by Indians and was often defended by only two companies.

WILD GAME RECIPES

Hunting fresh game along the trail provided the pioneers with variety in their meals and a means of stretching their precious supply of cured meats. The men soon learned that their guns had to be ready at all times, or they would miss their chance and suffer at mealtime.

Deer were the most common game animal along the trail. Antelope could be found on the high, bleak elevations of the western prairie and mountain foothills. Wild ducks, geese, turkey, prairie chickens, sage hens and rabbit provided a variety of small game for the traveling pioneers. Buffalo were plentiful on the prairie in the 1840's and supplied a valuable source of fresh meat. The tongue, hump and marrow bones were regarded as the choicest pieces of the buffalo.

The following section features game hunted by pioneers while traveling the Oregon Trail. Since buffalo and prairie chicken are difficult to find today, many of the wild game recipes are written for modern hunters and cooks.❖

WILD GAME RECIPES

BIG GAME

Venison should be bled immediately after the kill and hung for at least 48 hours. Season steaks and chops with garlic and/or red wine and broil rare. Braise the less tender cuts, brown in fat, add water, cover and cook until tender. Wine can be added to flavor. Roast the saddle as you would mutton, with wild rice dressing. Lard it if needed. Roasting time: 20-25 minutes per pound.

SOD BUSTER BUFFALO STEAK

Render some fat in a hot skillet. Add sirloin of buffalo steak and sear on both sides. At lower heat, cook as beefsteak until done. For gravy, add a tablespoon of flour to the pan drippings and cook until brown. Stirring constantly, add a cup of milk and bring to a boil. Salt to taste.

CHEYENNE BUFFALO JERKY

Slice buffalo meat along the grain into strips $1/8$ inch thick, $1/2$ inch wide and 2-3 inches long. Hang them on a rack in a pan and bake at 200° until dry. To prepare outside, suspend them over a fire or drape them on bushes to dry in the sun.

WILD GAME RECIPES

FRESH BUFFALO TONGUE

1 buffalo tongue
3 sprigs parsley
1 tsp. salt
1 onion
1 tsp. peppercorns
2 bay leaves

Wash the tongue; cover it with hot water. Add the seasonings. Simmer for 2 1/2-3 hours or until the meat is tender. Skin the tongue, slice and serve hot or allow it to cool in the liquid after skinning and serve cold. Make a stew from the meat at the base of the tongue, the liquid and serve with the meat which is not in shape for slicing.

BARLOW'S ANTELOPE STEW

2 lbs. antelope stew meat
1/4 c. oil or drippings
Boiling water or stock
1 c. onion, diced
2 tsp. salt
1/2 tsp. paprika
1 c. carrots, chunked
2 c. potatoes, chunked
2 T. lemon juice
1/2 tsp. Worcestershire sauce
1 minced garlic clove
2 bay leaves
1/4 tsp. pepper
1/8 tsp. cloves or allspice
6-8 sm. onions or wedges from 2-3 med. onions

Brown meat in drippings or oil in heavy pan. Add seasonings, garlic, onions and water or stock; cover. Simmer until meat is tender. Add vegetables and cook until done. Thicken the liquid with flour and water paste if you desire a thickened gravy.

WILD GAME RECIPES

OREGON TRAIL CHILI

(Made from Deer or Antelope)

1 lb. ground meat
1/2 lb. ground pork
2 med. onions
2 tsp. salt
Dash of cayenne pepper
1 tsp. ground cumin
2 T. chili powder mixed with 2 T. flour

Stir and fry ground meats until lightly brown. Add onion and stir and fry until brown. Add other ingredients. Cover with just enough water to cover meat. Cover and cook slowly for about an hour. Add pinto beans, if desired.

BLAZED BARBECUE DEER ROAST

1 c. ketchup
1 T. Worcestershire sauce
1 c. water
1 tsp. salt
2 T. vinegar or lemon juice
1 stick margarine
1 tsp. mustard
1 med. onion

Cook roast on top of stove until tender. Brown onion in margarine. Add ketchup and other ingredients and let come to boil. Cut roast in slices. Put in roast pan. Pour barbecue sauce over roast. Cover with foil and bake 1 hour at 350°.

WILD GAME RECIPES

POWDER HORN VENISON STEAKS

8 med.-sized venison steaks
2 c. chopped celery
2 c. chopped onions
2 c. flour

Flour and pan-fry steaks in 1 inch of oil until brown on both sides. In large baking dish, layer steaks, chopped onions and celery alternately. Pour thin gravy over top. Bake at 250° for 2 1/2 hours. Season to taste.

Thin Gravy Sauce:

1 T. meat drippings
2 c. milk
2 T. flour

Mix drippings and flour until smooth. Add milk and cook until mixture thickens slightly.

VENISON TENDERLOIN

1 whole venison tenderloin
1/4 lb. butter
1 med. onion, sliced
Worcestershire sauce
5 slices bacon, cooked but not crisp

As soon as deer is dressed and hung up to cool, cut out tenderloin by inserting knife blade along backbone with one hand while pulling meat away with the other hand. Trim all silverskin (membrane) and fat from meat. Cut into small steaks. In skillet over medium high heat, melt butter. Saute steaks with sliced onion, sprinkling with Worcestershire sauce. Wrap with bacon and serve with toothpick. Makes about 6 appetizer servings. If tenderloin is not available, any part of deer can be tenderized for this recipe by removing silverskin and fat and pounding with back of French knife blade. Preparation time: 2 hours. Serves 6.

WILD GAME RECIPES

SMOKED DEER HAM

5 to 8-lb. deer ham, trimmed neatly
1/2 c. Worcestershire sauce
1 c. Italian dressing
1 T. cayenne red pepper
1 T. salt
1 T. pepper
1 c. chopped onions
1/2 c. soft butter

Combine all ingredients in bowl; stir. Put ham in large container; cover with all the ingredients. Can slice holes in meat so it can soak inside better. Cover good; soak overnight or about 10 hours. Can turn over about 2 or 3 hours to marinate. Put on smoker and let smoke for 6 hours; turn and smoke 4 more hours or until tender.

VENISON BACKSTRAP (TENDERLOIN) WITH CREAM GRAVY

Deer backstrap, cut crosswise into 3/4-inch slices, allowing at
    least 3 or 4 slices per person
Vegetable oil (enough to deep fry meat), at least 1-2 inches deep
    in fryer
Flour, seasoned with: salt, pepper, garlic powder and oregano
    (enough flour to dust meat thoroughly and have some left over
    to make gravy, at least 1 c.)
3 or 4 cupfuls milk or more
About 1/2 stick margarine
About 1/4 c. vegetable oil

Flour meat thoroughly and deep fry 6 or 8 minutes or until golden brown. Meanwhile, in another pan, melt margarine. Add milk to melted margarine and bring to boil. Blend flour left over from flouring meat with 1/4 cup vegetable oil; then add this mixture to heated milk. Stir until smooth and thick, using a pancake turner for better stirring. Do not burn it; do not undercook and serve it raw.

WILD GAME RECIPES

WESTWARD SWISS STEAK

¹/₂ c. flour
Bacon drippings
2 lbs. venison steak
1 pkg. dry onion soup
2 c. canned tomatoes
2 bay leaves
2 T. sugar
¹/₄ c. green peppers, chopped
1 sm. jar mushrooms

Pound flour into meat. Cut meat into 1-inch thick strips. Brown meat quickly in small amount of bacon drippings. Drain off excess fat. Add remaining ingredients. Simmer slowly for 2 hours or until meat is tender. Salt and pepper not needed because the onion soup has enough.

ELK SWISS STEAK

Marinade:

1 can beer
1 garlic clove, minced
1 tsp. sugar
1 T. salt/pepper

Marinate steak for 1 day. Brown steak and place in covered casserole dish or a crockpot. Add chopped onion, celery and mushrooms. Add tomato sauce until meat is covered. Cook at 325° for 2-2 ¹/₂ hours or on low in crockpot.

We traveled over the most dreary country we had previously seen. The loose and hot sands were blown about in a manner most distressing to the mouth, nostrils, eyes and ears.
- Jessy Quinn, 1846

WILD GAME RECIPES

JERKED TRAIL MEAT
(Elk or Deer)

Lay meat and salt in alternating layers. Dissolve 1 cup brown sugar in water. Add the following spices:

1 tsp. allspice
1/2 tsp. red pepper
1 T. saltpeter

Pour over top of meat and let soak for 36 hours, then hang the meat up to dry.

WAGON MASTER MOOSE

2 1/2 lbs. moose steak, 1/2 inch thick
1/8 c. butter or margarine
1 c. chopped onion
1/2 clove garlic, minced
1/2 T. paprika
Dash of black pepper
2 cans mushroom soup
1/2 c. water
1 c. sour cream
3 c. cooked noodles

Slice moose steak into thin strips, about 1 inch long. Saute in butter. Stir in onion, garlic, paprika and pepper. Stir soup until smooth; slowly blend in water to make a smooth sauce. Add to meat. Cover meat; simmer for 1 hour or until meat is tender. Stir occasionally. Stir a little hot sauce into sour cream; stir sour cream into meat mixture. Do not boil. Serve 6 ounces stroganoff with 1/2 cup hot, cooked noodles. Preparation time: 1 1/2 hours. Serves 6.

WILD GAME RECIPES

SETTLER STROGANOFF

3-lb. moose steak, sliced into $1/2$-inch strips
2 c. sliced mushrooms
2 c. onions, sliced
2 garlic buds, minced
3 T. brandy
3 T. butter
2 tsp. tomato paste
3 tsp. tomato sauce
3 tsp. Dijon mustard
$1/2$ tsp. nutmeg
2 T. fresh dill, chopped
Black pepper
1 $1/2$ c. sour cream
$1/4$ c. sherry

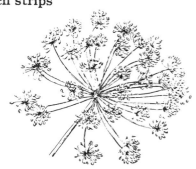

Heat butter and sear meat. Remove while still pink. Pour brandy into cooking pan and stir to get glazed. Add sliced mushrooms to pan with garlic and onions. Cook until soft. Then add other ingredients, blending gently. Top with dill. Serves 8.

MOOSE STEAK

Moose steak
$1/2$ c. onions, finely chopped
$1/2$ c. sweet or sour cream
1 c. chopped mushrooms
2 T. butter
2 T. flour

Fry onions; brown in butter. Sear steak on both sides in butter and browned onion. Cover and let simmer $1/2$ hour. When almost tender, stir the mushrooms and the flour into the cream and add to the meat. Cover and let simmer 20 minutes.

WILD GAME RECIPES

INDIAN SUMMER SAUSAGE

5 lbs. ground elk, antelope, venison or moose without suet
   added
5 tsp. rounded Morton's Tender Quick salt (required)
2 tsp. mustard seed
2 1/2 tsp. coarsely ground black pepper
2 1/2 tsp. garlic salt
1 tsp. smoked salt

Mix everything; cover and refrigerate overnight. Take mixture out
once a day for 3 days. Remix and return to refrigerator. On 4th day,
form into rolls approximately 18 inches long. Place rolls on broiler
rack. Place broiler pan of water under the rack of meat rolls. Bake
at 170-200° for 8 hours. After baking, rolls may be refrigerated for
immediate use or frozen for future use. Be sure to use a glass or
enamel bowl for the meat mixture. For a less salty and better eating product, use only 1/2 of the amount of salt called for.

BEAR LOIN BARBECUE-STYLE

3 lbs. bear tenderloins

Bear Sauce:

3/4 c. vinegar
3/4 c. ketchup
1 c. water
1 onion, chopped
1 clove garlic, minced
2 tsp. salt
1/4 tsp. pepper
1 T. Worcestershire sauce
1/4 tsp. Tabasco sauce
3 T. brown sugar
1 tsp. dry mustard

Slice meat in 1/2-inch pieces and cook for 30 minutes in a 350°
oven. Meanwhile, mix the sauce ingredients together in a saucepan.
Cook for 20 minutes over moderate heat. Pour off excess liquid from
meat; cover with barbecue sauce and cook at 350° for 1 hour.

WILD GAME RECIPES

SMALL GAME

Always dress at once and hang for 48 hours. Skin when ready for use. Rabbit is better flavored if dressed right after the kill and bled. Personal taste dictates whether or not you soak meat in vinegar, wine, salt water or not at all. Some methods of cooking: Rabbit pie with biscuit crust, southern fried, baked in milk with sage or baked with sour cream. Squirrel is mild, not gamey. Handle like rabbit, as to skinning, etc. Methods: Broil, southern fried or stew with dumplings.

PLOD-ALONG RABBIT

2 rabbits, cut up
Biscuit mix
2 tsp. poultry seasoning
Oil
1 can cream of chicken soup
1 can cream of mushroom soup
1 can water

Soak rabbit in salt water overnight; drain. Roll in biscuit mix and poultry seasoning. Fry in hot oil until brown. Place in slow cooker; add both cans of soup and 1 can of water. Cook for 4-6 hours or until meat is tender. **Note:** If slow cooker is in 2 pieces, heat on stove to warm before it is put on the base. If it has a dial, use 275°. Tame rabbit takes less time.

Everyone is busy preparing fires of buffalo chips to cook the evening meal, pitching tents and otherwise preparing for the night. . .
- Jesse Applegate, 1843

WILD GAME RECIPES

SWEETWATER MUSTARD RABBIT

1 lg. or 2 sm. rabbits
Flour
6 T. butter
3 T. olive oil
Mustard (Dijon or herb)
1 med. onion, finely chopped
1/2 c. chopped mushrooms
3 T. chopped parsley
Salt & pepper
1 c. heavy cream
Lemon juice (opt.)

Clean and cut rabbits into serving size portions. Soak in salted water 1-2 hours for young rabbit, overnight if older. Remove meat and pat dry. Dust with flour and saute in heavy skillet in butter and oil until brown on both sides. Remove and spread pieces very well with mustard. Place in shallow baking dish. Saute onion in remaining fat for several minutes. Add mushrooms and continue cooking. Add parsley, salt and pepper to taste. Blend in cream and heat through. Pour mixture over rabbit. Bake at 350° for 30-40 minutes or until tender. Taste sauce for salt. If desired, add a few drops of lemon juice. Serve with brown rice, cornbread and red cabbage. Serves 4.

WILD COUNTRY STYLE RABBIT

4 or 5 rabbit pieces
1/2 lb. turkey ham, cut into 1-inch squares
Freshly ground pepper
2 onions, peeled & chopped
3 carrots, peeled & chopped
1/2 tsp. Mrs. Dash salt-free herbs

Put foil in roasting pan. In center of foil, add rabbit pieces and cover with Shake 'N Bake for chicken. Add turkey ham, onions and carrots. Add mixed herbs, salt and pepper. Add 2 tablespoons water; fold sides of foil up and tuck in edges to cover. Bake in moderately hot 375° oven for 1 1/2 hours. Serves 4. This also bakes well on the shelf of your gas grill. Heat turned on low, lid closed.

WILD GAME RECIPES

SQUIRREL SOUP WITH DUMPLINGS

2 squirrels, skinned & cleaned
Salt & pepper to taste
1 egg, beaten slightly
1/2 pt. milk
Salt & pepper to taste
Water to cover
Flour
1 T. butter
1 T. lemon rind
Dash of nutmeg
Dash of mace
1 T. fresh parsley
1/2 pt. sweet cream

Thoroughly clean and skin the squirrels; cut into small pieces. Rinse and season with salt and pepper. Put meat into a large pot with water and boil until nearly done. Beat egg and stir it into the milk. Add a little more salt and pepper and enough flour to make a stiff batter. Drop by teaspoonfuls into the soup. Cook dumplings with meat until done. Then stir in butter, rolled in flour, lemon rind, mace and nutmeg. Add parsley and cream; stir until it comes to a boil. Serve with squirrel. Instead of squirrel, try chicken, rabbit, pigeon, pheasant, turkey, etc.

WILD GAME RECIPES

SQUIRREL, SMOKED

Marinate squirrels overnight in:

1 c. water
1 c. red wine
$1/2$ c. salt
4 T. sugar
$1/2$ tsp. pepper
1 tsp. crushed garlic
1 T. crushed onion
1 T. MSG

The following day, place pieces on cookie sheet to air dry for a couple hours. Put in electric smoker for 2 hours (2 pans of smoke). Place in a 225° oven to finish off, basting with butter for 2 more hours.

OSAGE ORANGE SQUIRREL ROAST

2 dressed squirrels, quartered
1 c. orange juice
2 bay leaves
8 strips bacon
2 carrots, chopped
1 c. white wine
1 onion, chopped
1 unpeeled orange, sliced

Wrap the squirrel quarters in bacon strips, securing them with wooden toothpicks, and place in a roasting pan. Then add the carrots, onion, bay leaves, orange slices and wine. Place the roasting pan in a preheated 350° oven and let it cook, uncovered, for one half hour. Now pour the orange juice in the roaster pan and let it cook for one hour or until tender.

WILD GAME RECIPES

WESTERN FRIED SQUIRREL

2 dressed squirrels
1 (5-oz.) jar sliced mushrooms
1/2 stick margarine
4 T. water
1 c. sour cream
1 c. flour
1/2 tsp. salt
1/2 tsp. black pepper
1/2 c. sherry

Cut the dressed squirrels into serving portions and sprinkle with salt and pepper; then roll in the flour. Melt the margarine in a skillet over medium heat. Add the squirrel to the skillet; slowly fry and brown on all sides. Remove the done squirrel to a warm platter and make the gravy by adding 2 tablespoons flour and 2 tablespoons of water to the skillet, stirring until smooth and thickened. Now add the sour cream, sherry and drained mushrooms to the skillet. Stir until smooth, then pour the hot gravy over the golden brown squirrel and serve.

BIG BLUE BEAVER TAIL SOUP

Take two beaver tails and pour boiling water over them in a pan. The scales will come off. Wash well and put in a kettle and cook. They will dissolve into a thick broth. No bones much. Then add any vegetables you like or macaroni or beans; add seasoning to taste. This is a rich soup and an old trapper's stand by.

From six to seven o'clock is a busy time; breakfast is eaten, tents struck, wagons loaded, and teams yoked. There are 60 wagons in 15 divisions or platoons of four wagons each.
- Jesse Applegate, 1843

WILD GAME RECIPES

FISH

JIM BRIDGER'S CATFISH SUPREME

4 lg. farm-raised catfish fillets
Garlic salt
Pepper
Juice of 1 lemon
2 T. Worcestershire sauce
4 T. soy sauce
4 T. melted margarine
1 lg. clove garlic, minced
Lemon slices

Sprinkle catfish fillets with garlic salt and pepper; set aside for 1 hour. In a blender, add lemon juice, Worcestershire sauce, soy sauce, melted margarine and garlic; blend. Coat each fillet with blended mixture; garnish with lemon slices and place in baking dish. Preheat oven to 375° and bake, uncovered, for 20 minutes.

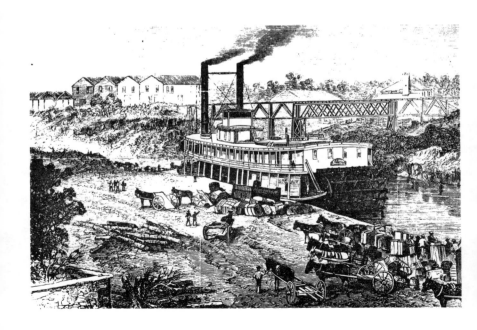

WILD GAME RECIPES

MUSTARD FRIED CATFISH

6 (10 to 12-oz.) catfish, cut into 1-inch strips
Vegetable oil
1/2 c. prepared yellow mustard
1 lg. egg, well beaten
1 tsp. Tabasco sauce
1/2 c. yellow cornmeal
1/4 c. all-purpose flour
1/4 c. Italian seasoned bread crumbs
1/4 tsp. garlic powder
1/4 tsp. paprika
1/2 tsp. salt
1/4 tsp. black pepper
1 lg. onion, sliced

In a medium bowl, combine mustard, egg and Tabasco sauce. In another bowl, combine all remaining ingredients except onion. Place fish in large baking dish. Pour mustard mixture over fish. Coat with cornmeal mixture. Gently place fish 2-3 at a time in preheated oil. Add sliced onion a few at a time. Fry until golden brown and crispy for 5-6 minutes on each side, turning once. Drain on paper towel. Yield: 4-6 servings.

. . . at length the pilot is standing ready to conduct the train into the circle 100 yards deep which he has marked out. So accurate the measurement and so perfect the practice, that the hindmost wagon always precisely closes the gateway. Within ten minutes from the time the leading wagon is halted, the barricade is formed.

- Jesse Applegate, 1843

WILD GAME RECIPES

PLATTE RIVER CATFISH FILLETS

2 T. lemon juice
2 T. white wine
1/2 c. dry bread crumbs
1/4 tsp. salt
1/8 tsp. garlic powder
1/8 tsp. pepper
1 lb. catfish fillets
2 tsp. oil

Heat oven to 450°. Spray 15 x 10 x 1-inch baking pan with non-stick cooking spray. In shallow dish, combine lemon juice and wine. In another shallow dish, combine bread crumbs, salt, garlic powder and pepper. Dip fillets in liquid, then dip in crumbs to coat. Arrange coated fillets on sprayed pan; drizzle with oil. Bake at 450° for 8-10 minutes or until fish flakes easily with fork. Makes 4 servings.

GOLDEN BROWN WALLEYE

1-3 lbs. walleye, perch or northern fillets
3 eggs
1/2 can warm beer
1 pkg. Pillsbury potato buds

Cut fillets of desired fish into 1-inch or 2-inch cubes. Beat the eggs and beer together in a large bowl and put fish fillets in this batter for 5 minutes. Roll or dip fillet chunks in the potato buds until well coated. Place fish in a deep fat fryer until golden brown.

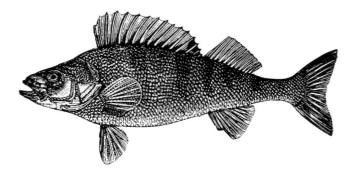

WILD GAME RECIPES

BAKED WILDERNESS WALLEYE

2 lbs. boned, skinned walleye fillets
Salt
1 c. sour cream
1 T. white vinegar
Dash of cayenne pepper
Lawry's seasoned pepper
1 T. instant onion flakes
1/4 tsp. celery seed

Sprinkle fillets with salt; season with seasoned pepper. Mix rest of ingredients. Place fillets in single layer in well greased baking pan. Pour over sour cream mixture. Sprinkle with paprika. Bake for 30-35 minutes. In microwave, cover with Saran Wrap and bake at high power for 7 minutes. If not ready, 2 more minutes.

WESTPORT WALLEYE FISH FRY

1 c. flour
1 tsp. sugar
1 tsp. baking powder
2 eggs
1/4 c. water
8 walleye fillets or any fish fillets
Vegetable oil for frying

Pat fillets dry and set aside. Combine all ingredients except vegetable oil and fillets; mix well. You will need more water. Add water until the mix drips steadily but does not run from fork. In a cast iron pan or deep fryer, heat at least 1 1/2 inches of vegetable oil until 360-370°. Dip fillets into mix; slide into oil and remove when brown. Serve immediately. **Note:** Maintain oil temperature. Small fillets work best or cut large fillets into 1/2 x 3-inch strips.

WILD GAME RECIPES

CARAVAN LEMON PERCH

$1/4$ c. butter
2 T. lemon juice
$1/2$ tsp. salt
$1/4$ tsp. dill weed
1 lb. perch fillets

Melt butter in skillet; stir in lemon juice and seasonings. Place fish in skillet skin side down; cook 4-5 minutes over medium heat. Turn; continue cooking until fish flakes easily with fork. Serve butter mixture over fish. Makes 4 servings.

TRAIL SIDE BULLHEADS

10 bullheads
1 $1/2$ c. dry white wine
3 T. lemon juice
3 T. parsley flakes
3 tsp. salt
1 c. vegetable oil
$1/2$ c. chopped onions
2 c. sliced mushrooms
$1/2$ tsp. pepper
$1/2$ tsp. thyme
2 crushed bay leaves

Cut 10 squares of heavy-duty aluminum foil, 18 inches square, and grease each lightly. Place 2 bullheads on each square of foil; then turn the edges up slightly. Mix together all of the ingredients to create a sauce; then pour an equal amount over each fish. Then fold the edges over to make tightly sealed packages and place on the grill about 6 inches above a bed of charcoal. Cook for 25-30 minutes or until the fish flakes easily. Serves 5.

WILD GAME RECIPES

NORTH PLATTE BAKED CARP

6 lbs. fish, split fish partially
2 tsp. lemon juice
2 onions
3 tsp. butter
1/2 tsp. pepper
1 tsp. salt
1/4 tsp. poultry seasoning

Put all ingredients inside of the fish. Cut up onions in quarters. Pour lemon juice inside fish. Add pepper and salt and butter. Sprinkle pepper and salt on outside. Sprinkle poultry seasoning on inside of fish. Baste fish after it starts to cook in 350° oven.

WILD GAME RECIPES

OREGON SALMON MOUSSE

1 env. plain gelatin
1/4 c. dry white wine or 1 c. Campbell's chicken stock
2 c. firmly packed salmon, fresh, cooked (simmer salmon in 1
    qt. water & 2 T. wine vinegar 12 minutes, drain)
2 tsp. tomato paste
1 tsp. paprika
1 T. finely grated onion
1 1/2 tsp. salt
1 T. lemon juice
1/8 tsp. Tabasco sauce
1/2 c. heavy cream

Soften gelatin in wine or chicken stock, until dissolved. Pour in
food processor or blender and add the cooked salmon. Blend until
pureed. Scrape into bowl. Add all other ingredients except cream.
Whip cream in a chilled bowl until firm but not stiff. Fold into
salmon mixture. Pour into molds.

Sauce:

1 egg, beaten until fluffy

Add:

1 tsp. salt
Pinch of pepper
4 tsp. lemon juice or dill pickle juice
1 tsp. grated onion
1 T. dill weed
1 1/2 c. sour cream

Mix all together well and serve over mousse.

WILD GAME RECIPES

END-OF-THE-TRAIL STUFFED SALMON

1 whole salmon
1 sm. onion, finely chopped
5 sliced mushrooms
4 T. butter
1 tsp. salt
Sprinkle of thyme
3 T. parsley
1 c. buttered bread crumbs
2 egg yolks
2 c. shrimp, fresh or canned or frozen
3 T. chopped fresh parsley
6 to 7 bacon slices
Dry red wine (Almaden or similar)

Saute onion in butter. Add mushrooms, salt, thyme, parsley. Combine with bread crumbs, shrimp, egg yolks. Stuff salmon and hold together with toothpicks. Place in well-oiled pan. Cut slashes in salmon through the skin; cover slash with bacon. Sprinkle salt and pepper. Pour 1 cup wine over top. Bake at 400°, allowing 10 minutes per pound. Baste frequently with more wine. Don't be surprised if it takes maybe 3/4 of the bottle. Could cover the top loosely with foil.

WILD GAME RECIPES

POACHED TROUT FILLETS

2 trout fillets
1 c. water
1 lg. piece aluminum foil, 4 inches longer than skillet width
1 T. lemon juice
1 T. soy sauce
1 T. dry sherry or water
Dash of sesame oil
6-8 slivers fresh ginger root, 2-3 inches long
2 green onions, cut into 2 to 3-inch long slivers
$1/2$ tsp. cornstarch dissolved in 1 $1/2$ tsp. cold water

Put 1 cup water in medium-sized skillet (oval saute pan is best). Place foil over top of skillet. Indent the middle of the foil into skillet, about halfway to bottom. Fold down sides of foil (keep it on the side so the flame does not burn it). Turn burner on high until steam escapes. Turn burner down to a medium heat that will maintain steam. Pour lemon juice, soy sauce, sherry and sesame oil into foil. Place fillets into liquid. Arrange ginger root slivers and green onion slivers loosely on top of each fillet. Cover skillet with lid or another piece of foil. Poach 3-4 minutes or until fillets flake easily and are still moist. **Do not overcook!** Remove fillets, ginger root and green onions. Discard ginger root. Place fillets on plate with green onions on top. Stir cornstarch mixture into lemon-soy-sherry mixture until thickens. Pour over fillets.

WILD GAME RECIPES

ROCKY MOUNTAIN BROILED TROUT

2 lbs. skinless trout
2 T. lemon juice
$1/2$ c. grated Parmesan cheese
$1/4$ c. margarine, softened
3 T. mayonnaise or salad dressing
3 T. chopped green onion
$1/4$ tsp. salt
Dash of liquid hot pepper sauce

Place fillets in a single layer on a well greased 10 x 16-inch bake-and-serve platter. Brush fillets with lemon juice and let stand 10 minutes. Combine remaining ingredients. Broil fillets about 4 inches from source of heat for 6-8 minutes or until fillets flake easily when tested with a fork. Remove from heat and spread with cheese mixture. Broil 2-3 minutes longer or until lightly browned. Makes 6 servings.

MOUNTAIN STREAM BAKED TROUT

4 med. trout
4 tsp. brown sugar
4 tsp. butter
Onion flakes
Lemon juice

Stuff cleaned trout with brown sugar, butter, onion flakes and lemon juice. Wrap fish in foil and place on cookie sheet. Bake at 350° for 35 minutes. Serves 4.

WILD GAME RECIPES

LITTLE BLUE FRIED FROG LEGS

2 lbs. frog legs
2 eggs, beaten
2 T. mayonnaise
1 T. cornstarch
1 T. lemon juice
1/2 tsp. baking powder
1/4 tsp. salt
1/8 tsp. pepper
2/3 c. all-purpose flour
1/3 c. seasoned dry bread crumbs
Vegetable oil

Arrange frog legs in shallow container. Combine eggs and next 6 ingredients. Stir until smooth. Pour over legs and cover and chill for at least 30 minutes. Combine flour and bread crumbs in plastic bag. Remove legs from the marinade, shaking off excess; place 2 legs at a time in the flour mixture. Close bag and shake until well coated. Pour oil 2-3 inches deep in Dutch oven and heat to 375°. Fry legs 1-2 minutes or until dark golden brown; drain on paper towels. You can substitute orange roughy or peeled shrimp for the frog legs.

WILD GAME RECIPES

LONE PRAIRIE TURTLE BURGERS

2 lbs. turtle meat, ground
$1/2$ green peppers, minced
1 stalk celery, minced
1 tsp. salt
1 tsp. black pepper
2 eggs, beaten
2 onions, minced
1 tsp. garlic powder
1 tsp. parsley flakes
1 c. bread crumbs
2 tsp. Worcestershire sauce

Mix all ingredients together in a large mixing bowl; then shape the mixture into thick burger patties. Next, the burgers may be cooked over medium coals on a grill as desired, or fried in a skillet with cooking oil.

FOWL

Birds should be plump, fat and firm. They should be plucked and singed to keep maximum flavor. They do not require long hanging. They are excellent when roasted on a split, sauteed in butter, broiled, or they may be poached in strong veal stock with white wine. Brandy or a dash of lemon is flavorful. They are further set off with mushrooms, bacon slices, sour cream, diced ham, truffles, sweet bread, celery and Madeira sauce. Among fruits, cherries, pomegranate, oranges, pineapples, apples and white grapes may be included in the processing.

WILD GAME RECIPES

PRAIRIE CHICKENS WITH RED CABBAGE

2 prairie chickens or grouse
1 can red cabbage
1/2 pt. sour cream
4 shallots, chopped
4 slices bacon

Stuff grouse with red cabbage, sour cream and shallot mixture. Cover breasts with bacon slices. Roast at 350° for 1 hour, basting often with white wine.

PRAIRIE CHICKEN SUPREME

6-8 prairie chickens
4 T. margarine
1 stalk celery, chopped
1 sm. can mushrooms, drained
1 1/2 c. uncooked rice
1 can onion soup
2 c. boiling water
Salt & pepper to taste

Saute celery, mushrooms and rice in margarine until brown. Place in roaster or 9 x 9-inch pan. Mix water and soup and pour over rice. Butter the quail and place on top of rice. Add salt and pepper. Bake at 350° for about 1 hour, covered. Baste occasionally with liquid from pan.

At the nooning place, the teams are not unyoked, but simply turned loose from the wagon. Today an extra session of the Council is being held to settle a dispute between a proprietor and a young man who has undertaken to do a man's service on the journey for bed and board. The high court, from which there is no appeal, will define the rights of each party.
- Jesse Applegate, 1843

WILD GAME RECIPES

BAKED PRAIRIE CHICKEN

1 qt. water
1 T. salt
4 prairie chicken breasts
1 onion
1 can cream of mushroom or chicken soup
Pepper
Rice or noodles

Soak breasts in salt water overnight (1 quart water to 1 tablespoon salt). Drain birds. Place in casserole, breast down. Slice 1 onion over birds. Pour 1 can soup over birds and onion. Pepper to taste. Cover and cook at 350° for 1 1/2 hours or until meat comes away from the bone. Serve over rice or noodles.

WILD GAME RECIPES

SMALL-GAME ROUND-UP

6 pheasant legs, 6 grouse, 3 squirrels or 1 rabbit
1 c. dry red wine
1 tsp. sugar
1/4 c. wine vinegar
1/8 tsp. garlic powder
Pinch of red pepper
2 T. butter
2 T. cooking oil
1 onion, sliced
Flour
Salt & pepper
2 T. tomato paste
1 c. sm. whole mushrooms
Hot, buttered rice

Put the wine, sugar, vinegar, garlic powder and red pepper in a saucepan and heat to the boiling point. Cool slightly. Place the game pieces in a nonmetal bowl and cover with the marinade. Add a little water, if necessary, to cover the game. Marinate for 4 hours, turning the game once. Heat the butter and cooking oil in a large frying pan; then fry the onion over medium heat for 5 minutes. Push the onion slices up the sides of the pan. Remove the game from the marinade and dry on paper towels. Roll in the flour seasoned with a little salt and pepper. Brown on all sides in hot butter and oil over medium high heat. Add tomato paste to the marinade and blend. Add the mixture to the pan and bring to a boil. Turn the game pieces and onion over in the mixture. Add the mushrooms; cover and turn the heat to simmer. Cook until tender. Serves 4. Spoon the meat and sauce over hot, buttered rice and serve with green salad and hot rolls.

WILD GAME RECIPES

WAGON WHEEL QUAIL PIE

6 quail
3 c. self-rising flour
Ice water
3 T. melted butter
Milk
2 c. water
1 c. shortening
Salt & pepper to taste
2 T. flour

Pressure cook quail 25 minutes in 2 cups water. Make a pastry of flour, shortening and ice water for a stiff dough. Roll out 1/2 the dough. Cover the bottom of large casserole. Place cooked, boned quail in casserole. Salt and pepper and pour melted butter over meat. Thicken quail broth with 2 tablespoons flour and pour over quail. Roll remaining dough thin, cut into strips; prick well. Place a few strips over quail, bringing ends to meet bottom pastry. Brush with milk and bake at 350° for 40 minutes.

WILD GAME RECIPES

FIRESIDE SMOKED QUAIL

24 quail
1/3 c. white vinegar
1 T. dried sage
1 T. chopped oregano
1 T. Worcestershire sauce
2 garlic cloves, minced
1/4 tsp. dried thyme
1 tsp. sugar
1 1/2 c. vegetable oil
Salt & pepper
24 slices thin bacon

Pat quail dry. Arrange in a single layer in a non-aluminum container. In a mixing bowl, combine vinegar, sage, oregano, Worcestershire sauce, garlic, thyme, sugar and whisk in oil very slowly. Pour marinade over quail. Cover and refrigerate several hours or overnight, turning occasionally. Drain quail; salt and pepper and wrap each quail in bacon, securing with toothpicks. Arrange quail on grill; cover and smoke until leg bones move easily. Turn occasionally.

WILD GAME RECIPES

QUAIL COOK-IN-A-BAG

1 T. flour
1 lg. oven cooking bag
6 quail
Salt & pepper to taste
1 c. onion, chopped
1/2 c. green pepper, chopped
1 lb. fresh mushrooms, sliced
1 bay leaf
1 c. dry sherry
Juice of 1/2 lemon
1 c. water

Grease a large roasting pan. Put flour in oven cooking bag and shake, making sure that the inside of bag is evenly coated. Split birds lengthwise in half and sprinkle flesh with salt and pepper. Place birds in the bag and add the onion, green pepper, mushrooms, bay leaf, sherry, lemon juice and water. Tie the bag and punch 12 holes in the top of the bag. Roast at 350° for 45 minutes. This method of roasting creates its own gravy and bastes the birds at the same time.

. . . The caravan has been about two hours in motion. . . near the bank of the shining river is a company of horsemen. A member. . . has raised a flag. . . a signal for the wagons to steer their course to where he stands. The wagons form a line three quarters of a mile in length; some of the teamsters ride upon the front of their wagons, some walk beside their teams; scattered along the line companies of women and children are taking exercise on foot; they gather bouquets of rare and beautiful flowers along the way.

- Jesse Applegate, 1843

WILD GAME RECIPES

GRILLED QUAIL WITH ROSEMARY

8 ready-to-cook quail
$1/4$ c. olive oil
2 T. lemon juice
1 tsp. fresh rosemary leaves
$1/4$ tsp. salt
$1/8$ tsp. pepper
Rosemary sprigs

Rinse and thoroughly drain quail. If using charcoal grill, start charcoal. In a large bowl, combine olive oil, lemon juice, rosemary, salt and pepper; add quail. Set aside to marinate for 30 minutes, turning birds occasionally so that each is well coated with marinade. Arrange quail on 2 long skewers or on the spit of a charcoal grill. Grill 4 inches from heat, basting frequently with marinade for 15-25 minutes, depending upon intensity of heat. When roasted over medium coals on a spit, or on frequently turned skewers placed on a rack, quail will be thoroughly cooked in about 15 minutes. Quail are done when legs may be easily moved. Garnish with fresh rosemary. Marinated quail may also be roasted in a preheated 450° oven for 15-20 minutes.

WILD GAME RECIPES

FUR TRADER'S STUFFED QUAIL

12 quail
12 thin slices bacon
2 sticks margarine
1 lb. pork sausage
2 c. flour
3 T. grape jelly
2 c. red wine

Stuff each quail with sausage. Wrap a strip of bacon around each quail's breast; secure with toothpick. Season the flour with salt and pepper. Roll quail in seasoned flour. Melt 2 sticks of margarine in frying pan. Place quail in frying pan and brown. Remove quail from pan. Add enough seasoned flour to drippings to make enough brown gravy to cover birds. Add wine and grape jelly. Place quail in deep pan or baking dish. Pour gravy over quail. Cover container. Bake in slow oven (about 250°) until tender, about 1 1/2-2 hours.

PRAIRIE SCHOONER DOVES

Doves
Salt & pepper to taste
Flour
Butter or oleo

Generously salt and pepper doves. Dust with flour. Melt butter or oleo in skillet and brown doves on both sides. Remove doves to baking dish. Add water to pan drippings and pour over doves. Cover tightly with foil and bake in slow 300° oven for 2 hours. Gravy is delicious over rice.

WILD GAME RECIPES

OVER-THE-FIRE DOVES

2-3 doves per person

Baste with the following ingredients:

Juice of 2-3 lemons
2 T. brown sugar
1 T. salt
Dash of pepper

Cook on a covered charcoal grill for approximately 30 minutes while basting with the mixture above. Doves should be pink and not overdone, therefore cooking time may vary from grill to grill.

WEST BOUND BARBECUED DOVES

12-24 doves

Marinade:

2 c. vegetable oil
1/4 c. Worcestershire sauce
1/4 c. vinegar
2 T. salt
1 T. cracked black pepper
5-6 dashes Tabasco
Juice of 4 lemons
3-4 T. commercial barbecue sauce
Bacon slices

Marinate doves at least overnight (24 hours won't be too long). Drain and wrap each one with half slice of bacon (secure with toothpick). Cook over whitened coals on the grill 40 minutes to an hour, basting with marinade occasionally.

WILD GAME RECIPES

IRON SKILLET-ROASTED DOVES

2 T. all-purpose flour
1/2 tsp. salt
1 tsp. black pepper
20 dove breasts
2 T. margarine, melted
2 T. bacon drippings
1 c. dry red wine, divided
1 1/2 c. chicken broth, divided
1 T. red currant jelly
2 T. all-purpose flour

Combine first 3 ingredients; dredge doves in mixture. Brown doves on both sides in margarine and bacon drippings in a large skillet. Gradually add 1/2 cup wine, 3/4 cup broth and jelly. Cover and cook over low heat for 40 minutes. Remove dove and keep warm. Combine 2 tablespoons flour, remaining 1/2 cup red wine and remaining 3/4 cup broth, stirring until flour dissolves. Gradually add flour mixture to the pan drippings. Cook over medium heat, stirring constantly, until mixture thickens. Serve the gravy with doves.

WILD GAME RECIPES

DOVES IN RED WINE

12 doves (the bag limit)
Salt & pepper
1 lg. onion, chopped
2/3 c. dry red wine
1 1/4 c. water
2 chicken bouillon cubes
2 ribs celery, cut in half
1 green bell pepper, halved
1 T. cornstarch

Salt and pepper birds. Brown birds in butter in pressure cooker without the top. Remove birds; saute onion in some butter and add doves. Add wine, water, bouillon cubes, celery and pepper. Cover pressure cooker and cook 15 minutes at 10 pounds of pressure. Cool off cooker; open slowly. Remove doves, discard celery and pepper. Mix cornstarch with 1/4 cup cold water and add to juices in cooker and warm with top off. Without pressure cooker, simmer doves 2 hours in Dutch oven with similar results. Serve over rice.

DOVE RISOTTO

6 slices bacon
1 med. onion, chopped
1 1/2 c. uncooked reg. rice
1 bay leaf
Pinch of dried whole thyme
12 dove breasts
5 c. chicken broth
1 T. dried parsley flakes
1/8 tsp. hot sauce
1 (4-oz.) can sliced mushrooms, drained

Cook bacon in a large skillet until crisp; remove bacon, reserving drippings in skillet. Crumble bacon and set aside. Brown dove breasts in skillet. Add onion; saute 2 minutes. Add remaining ingredients except mushrooms; cover and cook over low heat 25 minutes or until rice is tender, stirring once. Remove bay leaf; add mushrooms and cook 2 minutes or until thoroughly heated. Yields 4 servings.

WILD GAME RECIPES

ROAST DUCK WITH ORANGE SAUCE

Duck:

1 (4 to 5-lb.) duck
1 orange, sliced into quarters
Salt
Pepper
Poultry seasoning

Sauce:

1/2 c. sugar
1 T. wine vinegar
Juice of 2 oranges
1 bay leaf
1/2 tsp. thyme leaves
Grand Marnier, to taste
1 orange peel, grated
1 orange peel, cut into julienne strips

Cook julienne strips in scant amount of water until tender (5 minutes). In a heavy saucepan, combine sugar and wine vinegar. Cook over medium heat until sugar melts and begins to caramelize. Add the juice of 2 oranges, Grand Marnier and grated orange peel. Mix well and cook for 5 minutes. Add julienne strips. Season to taste and pour over duck. **Duck:** Preheat oven to 425°. Wash duck in cold water and remove excess fat. Season the inside cavity and outside of duck with salt, pepper and poultry seasoning. Place orange quarters inside duck and place duck in shallow roasting pan. Bake for 30 minutes. Remove duck from oven and pierce breast with heavy tine fork to drain grease. Turn oven down to 300° and bake duck for 60-75 additional minutes until tender.

WILD GAME RECIPES

DUCK & WILD RICE TRAIL CASSEROLE

2-lb. wild ducks
4 stalks celery
1 lg. onion, halved
Salt & pepper
1 (6-oz.) pkg. long grain & wild rice
1 (4-oz.) can sliced mushrooms
$1/2$ c. chopped onion
$1/2$ c. melted oleo
$1/4$ c. all-purpose flour
$3/4$ c. half-and-half
$3/4$ c. white wine
2 T. chopped fresh parsley
$1/2$ c. slivered almonds

Cook ducks with seasonings (celery, onion, salt and pepper), covered with water in Dutch oven for 1 hour or until tender. Remove ducks from stock. Let cool; strain stock and reserve. Cut meat into bite-sized pieces and set aside. Cook rice according to directions on package. Drain mushrooms, reserving liquid. Add enough duck broth (stock) to make 1 ½ cups. Saute chopped onion in oleo until tender; add flour, stirring until thick and smooth. Gradually stir in mushroom broth liquid. Cook over medium heat, stirring constantly, until thick and bubbly. Stir in duck, rice, half-and-half, wine and parsley. Spoon into a greased 2-quart shallow casserole. Sprinkle almonds on top. Cover and bake at 350° for 15-20 minutes until liquid is absorbed. Let rest 5 minutes before serving. Serves 6-8. You may substitute 3 cups cooked chicken for duck.

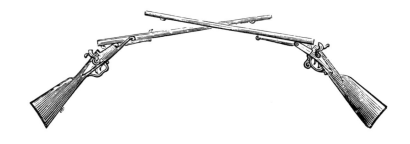

WILD GAME RECIPES

WAGON TRAIN WILD DUCK

4 wild wood ducks
4 apples
3 lg. onions
4 celery ribs with tops
4 T. butter, softened
Salt & ground pepper
$3/4$ c. brandy
$3/4$ c. currant jelly

Clean and dry ducks, inside and out. Stuff each duck with a piece or two of apple, onion and celery. Brush all with softened butter. Rub the duck well with butter and season with salt and pepper. Melt the currant jelly; combine with brandy and baste duck. Place ducks in large roasting pan on a rack and roast at 400°, basting with currant jelly mixture every 10 minutes. Cook 35-40 minutes for rare, 45-60 minutes for medium. Transfer to serving plate and pour over the pan juices.

BLAZING DUCK

2 ducklings, about 4 lbs. each
$1/4$ c. sherry wine
$1/4$ c. soy sauce
$1/4$ tsp. ground ginger
2 T. lemon juice
Salt & pepper
$1/2$ c. onions, chopped
$1/2$ c. celery, chopped
1 apple, chopped

Prepare hot coals. Season duckling with salt and pepper. Fill cavities with a mixture of onions, celery and apple. Clip off wing tips. Run spit through birds lengthwise, catching the bird in the fork of the wishbone. Cook on a rotisserie until tender, about 2 hours. Brush with a mixture of sherry, soy sauce, ginger and lemon juice during the last half hour of cooking. Serves 8.

WILD GAME RECIPES

WILLIAM H. JACKSON'S WILD DUCK

3 or 4 ducks
3 eggs
1 c. bread crumbs
Butter and bacon drippings
1 tsp. salt
1 tsp. pepper
1/4 tsp. paprika
2 bay leaves
4 whole cloves
2 cloves garlic, minced
1/4 c. Regina wine vinegar
1/2 c. catsup
2 T. Lea & Perrins
1 T. A-1 sauce
1 tsp. Kitchen Bouquet
1/2 c. burgundy wine
1 glass red currant jelly

Fillet the breast; if large, cut in 3 or 4 pieces lengthwise. Use only breasts and legs of ducks. Dip in beaten eggs, then into bread crumbs mixed with salt and pepper. Brown on all sides in butter and bacon drippings. Add everything except wine and jelly, mixed together in small bowl with some water. Simmer at least 1 hour or until tender. Add wine and jelly the last 10 minutes. Serve with rice. Serves 8. Also good with chicken breasts.

WILD GAME RECIPES

RIVER ROAST WILD GOOSE

1 young wild goose (about 10 lbs.) with giblets
Salt & pepper
8 med. onions, peeled
2-3 branches fresh sage or 1 tablespoon dried sage, crushed
8 thick slices fatty bacon
2 T. flour
1 c. strong stock made from giblets

Preheat oven to 325°. Rinse goose, drain and pat dry with paper towels, inside and out. Sprinkle cavity and all surfaces with salt and pepper. With a sharp knife, cut a quarter inch deep X in the root end of each onion. Fill goose body with the onions and the fresh or dried sage. Close the cavity and tie legs together with butchers cord. Place in roasting pan on rack, breast side up. Cover with the bacon slices and roast for about 2 hours. Remove bacon strips and dust goose with half of the flour. Continue roasting until crisp and done, about 30 minutes more. Transfer to heated platter and keep warm. Skim fat from pan juices and add remaining flour to juices, stirring over medium heat until smooth and thickened. Add stock slowly, stirring. Bring to boil and adjust seasoning with salt and pepper to taste. Serve on side as sauce. Serves 6. Serve with hot applesauce and baby Brussels sprouts.

WILD GAME RECIPES

GREAT AMERICAN GRILLED GOOSE

2 goose breast fillets
1 stick butter or oleo
Fat bacon
Lemon wedge
Spices: salt, pepper, cajun seasonings, garlic salt, soy sauce

Combine butter, lemon juice and selected seasonings in small saucepan and heat over low flame. Set aside. Wash breast fillets, removing skin and any damaged meat. With a sharp knife, cut fillets lengthwise, parallel to cutting board. You should now have 4 fillets of equal size, each approximately 1-1 1/2 inches thick. Wrap each fillet in fat bacon and secure with toothpicks. With grill at medium heat, place fillets on rack. Brush with butter and spices. Turn only once, basting occasionally. **Note:** You may use any one of the spices listed or any of your choice.

ROAST GOOSE WITH MUSHROOM GRAVY

1 (5 to 8-lb.) goose
Garlic salt
Paprika
1 1/2 stalks celery, chopped
1 carrot, chopped
1 med. onion, chopped
4 T. flour
1/2 tsp. rosemary
1/4 tsp. thyme
1 1/4 tsp. salt
1 c. sour cream
1 can mushrooms, drained

Season goose inside and out with garlic salt and paprika. Place on rack in shallow pan and bake, uncovered, for 1 hour in 325° oven. Boil giblets in water until tender. Cook celery, carrots and onion in small amount of fat until soft. Stir in 2 tablespoons flour and 1 cup stock from giblets. Add rosemary, thyme and salt. Stir remaining flour into the sour cream and blend into gravy. Remove goose from shallow pan; place in roasting pan and pour gravy mixture and mushrooms over goose. Cover and bake an additional 2 hours or until tender.

WILD GAME RECIPES

OVERLAND ORANGE GOOSE

1 wild goose
1 sm. orange
1 sliced apple
2 onion slices
Chopped celery
Melted butter

Clean and pick goose well, but do not skin. Stuff cavity of bird, starting with slices of orange, apple, onion, celery and ending with end of orange to close cavity. Baste top of bird with butter, then salt and pepper. Cover and roast in 350° oven until done, basting regularly with pan juices. Allow about 15-20 minutes per pound. Serve on hot platter.

SAGE BRUSH ROASTED GOOSE

Stuffing:

1/4 c. butter
1/2 c. celery, minced
1 pkg. Uncle Ben's long grain and wild rice, cooked according to directions
2 med. onions, minced
1 c. seedless grapes, sliced
1 tsp. salt

Saute onions with butter and add other ingredients. Rub bird with salt and pepper inside and outside. Stuff bird; put in brown-in-cooking bag. Bake 3-3 1/2 hours at 325° or until done.

WILD GAME RECIPES

PRAIRIE ROASTED WILD TURKEY

1 wild turkey (8-10 lbs.)
Salt & pepper
1/2 lb. sausage meat
1/2 c. finely chopped onion
1 c. finely chopped celery stalks
1 tsp. salt
1/4 tsp. pepper
1/2 tsp. crushed thyme
1/4 tsp. chervil
1/4 c. chopped fresh parsley
1 c. coarsely chopped, cooked chestnuts
1 stick melted butter or margarine
8 c. bread crumbs made from day-old bread
8 thick slices fatty bacon
1/2 c. melted bacon fat

Preheat oven to 325°. Rinse and dry turkey inside and out. Sprinkle cavity and skin with salt and pepper. In a large skillet, cook sausage meat until thoroughly done. Add the onion and celery and cook until glossy and translucent. Add salt, pepper, thyme, chervil, parsley and chestnuts. Stir through and transfer to large mixing bowl. Toss in bread crumbs and lightly mix. Add the melted butter and mix again lightly, turning the mixture with a fork. Fill neck and body with stuffing (do not pack too tightly; put extra stuffing in heavy aluminum foil, seal and bake in oven along with bird). Close cavities with skewers, or sew up. Place turkey on rack in roasting pan, breast side up. Tie legs together; turn wings under. Cover breast with bacon slices and ends of legs with foil. Soak a piece of cheesecloth in the melted bacon fat and place over bacon-covered breast. Roast for 20-25 minutes per pound or until done to taste. Baste frequently with fat and pan drippings. Serves 8. Serve with giblet gravy, buttered parsnips, cornbread, cranberry sauce and baked or whipped yams.

WILD GAME RECIPES

FRIED WILD TURKEY BREAST

Wild turkey breast, cut into strips
Flour
Salt
Pepper
Garlic powder
Worcestershire sauce

Remove breast from wild turkey. Boil rest of turkey to be used later. Season to taste with salt, pepper, and garlic powder. Put in a large bowl; add Worcestershire sauce. Cover and let set in refrigerator overnight. Dredge in flour. Deep fry until golden brown. Yield: 8-10 servings.

WHITMAN'S FRIED TURKEY

1 (12 to 16-lb.) turkey
1 sm. bottle Italian salad dressing, strained
1 tsp. salt
1 tsp. black pepper
1 tsp. red pepper
2 gal. low temp. peanut oil
2 T. garlic juice
1 baster with needle

Mix and strain Italian dressing and garlic juice. Add salt and pepper in a jar to measure 1 cup. Inject the marinade into the flesh of the turkey, especially the breast. Heat oil in large pot (18 to 20-quart) to 350°. Pot should be large enough to fit turkey and have oil cover it completely. Very carefully lower turkey into hot oil. Fry 1 hour for 14-pound turkey, slightly longer for larger bird. Let turkey sit on paper towels for 20 minutes before carving.

WILD GAME RECIPES

SETTLER ROAST TURKEY

8 or 10-lb. turkey
1 tsp. salt
Dash of garlic
1 egg
Dash of pepper on turkey
$^1/_8$ tsp. pepper
2 c. seasoned bread slices
1 c. celery
1 apple, cored, peeled & chopped

Preheat oven to 350°. Remove any excess fat from turkey. Sprinkle salt in cavity and rub over skin on turkey. Place in shallow roasting pan. Mix bread with garlic, egg and pepper. Stir in celery and apple. Fill cavity of turkey. Cover turkey with foil. Roast 2 hours. Uncover; roast 30 minutes longer or until turkey is brown and tender. Let turkey stand 15 minutes before carving.

Recipe Favorites

PUTTING UP ON THE TRAIL

Pickled,
preserved,
smoked,
dried,
or store it
in a hide.

CROSSING THE SOUTH PLATTE

Travelers arrived at the crossing point of the Platte River after traveling some 460 miles west of Missouri, and being on the trail at least a month. Wagons first had to cross the south fork in order to reach the north fork, which the trail followed. The river could be a half mile to a mile wide, depending on where it was crossed.

At times of high water, wagon wheels were removed and the wagon box sealed and floated across the river. A common way to waterproof the boxes was to cover the outside with buffalo hides. Even when the water was lower, pioneers still encountered difficulties, such as quicksand and sudden, deep holes. It usually required at least 45 minutes for a team of four to six animals to cross the South Platte River.

PUTTING UP ON THE TRAIL

Preserving and packing food was one of the most important preparations for the journey West. Nourishment was not the only criteria for selecting provisions. Foods had to be put up in the most secure, compact and portable manner possible. Jars and crocks did not travel well, thus dried fruits and vegetables were preferred to canned or pickled foods.

Dried foods were prepared by cutting the fresh food into thin slices and pressing them together very tightly to remove all the juices. These solid "cakes" were then thoroughly dried in an oven, becoming hard like bricks. When boiled, a small piece of the "cake", about the size of a child's hand, would be enough to serve four adults. The recipes found in this section are a combination of foods prepared for the journey and after the pioneers settled into their new homes.❖

PUTTING UP ON THE TRAIL

PIONEER WILD PLUM BUTTER

Wash fruit and cook with water barely covering the fruit. When tender, press through a colander to remove seeds. Using equal amounts of fruit pulp and sugar, cook until it begins to thicken. Put into jars and seal. In pioneer days before sealing wax was available, the women would put the butter into gallon stone jars, lay a piece of brown paper over the top and sprinkle sugar around the edges to seal.

TO PRESERVE WILD PLUMS

Gather plums when fully ripe, put in barrels, jars, tubs, or anything else that will hold water; cover them with water after filling up. There forms a scum on the top which keeps them from the air. They need no careful sealing or anything but a safe place from freezing during the winter, although it is advisable to weight down the lid.

PLUM SAUCE

Use small sour plums; four pounds of sugar and one and a half pints of vinegar to seven pounds of fruit. Tie up one ounce each of whole cloves and stick cinnamon in muslin bags and boil in the vinegar for ten minutes. Add the sugar and fruit and simmer slowly for several hours until it becomes very thick. Stir frequently to prevent burning. This is an excellent sauce for cold meat or roast ducks or game of any kind and will keep for several years.

APPLE BUTTER ON OPEN FIRE

Pare and core 12 bushels of apples. Add 16 gallons cider. Boil down, stirring constantly, until thickened. Cook all day on an open fire in an iron kettle. Add spices.

PUTTING UP ON THE TRAIL

CONESTOGA CURRANT JELLY

Strip the currants off the stem and bruise them thoroughly; put on the fire to heat and when at boiling point, strain them. To a pint of juice, allow a pound of loaf sugar. When the mixture begins to boil again, let it boil just fifteen minutes.

CORN COB SYRUP

One dozen large, clean red cobs. Cover these with water; boil one to two hours. Drain off the water and strain it. There should be a pint of it. Add two pounds of brown sugar to this and boil to desired thickness.

OLD FASHIONED CROCK PICKLES

2 qts. cider vinegar
1 med. sized onion, washed, peeled & sliced
2 T. dry mustard
2 T. salt
$^1/_2$ oz. white ginger root
2 T. whole cloves
2 (3-inch) sticks cinnamon, broken
1 T. whole peppercorns
1 T. powdered cloves
$^1/_2$ lb. (1 $^3/_8$ c. packed) brown sugar
2 qts. midget cucumbers, washed & drained

Mix all ingredients, except cucumbers, together in a 1-gallon crock or large glass jar. Add cucumbers. Cover crock or jar with folded cheesecloth, then with lid. Let stand in cool, dark place at least 1 month before using. Better if allowed to stand 3 months. Makes 2 quarts pickles.

PUTTING UP ON THE TRAIL

HOT-ON-THE-TRAIL HORSERADISH

This is a plant that is usually found in low, damp ground. The roots may be dug up. Tops may be cut off and replanted. The roots, 1/4 inch in size and larger, may be taken in, peeled, thick skin removed and rotten parts removed, washed and then run through a grinder. This should be done on a warm day where doors and windows can be opened. After being ground, place in jar. Cover with vinegar. Place lid on. Use sparingly on meats or in stews or beans.

PREPARED HORSERADISH

2 c. ground horseradish
3/4 c. vinegar
3/4 c. light cream
1 tsp. salt
1 tsp. sugar

Wash and shred (coarse) horseradish. Pour vinegar over top. Mix cream, salt and sugar. Stir into horseradish. Store in crocks or jars with lids.

(I) took my departure from Independence, Mo., in company with two hundred others, their wagons and the necessary teams, for the long, and, . . uncertain journey across the Plains. The destination of the party was Oregon.
- Samuel Hancock, 1845

PUTTING UP ON THE TRAIL

SOUTH PASS SAUERKRAUT

Use wooden tub or stone jar. Slice the cabbage fine. Place a layer of clean cabbage leaves on the bottom of the container. Sprinkle over them a small handful of salt and put in a layer of cut cabbage, about six inches in depth. Sprinkle over the cabbage a small handful of salt and by means of a wooden beetle or the end of a round stick of hard wood, pound the cabbage until juice appears (do not pound salt too much). Now add another small handful of salt, then pound, and continue this process until the container is nearly full. Cover the top over with clean cabbage leaves and lay over these several thicknesses of cheesecloth. Place a clean board or plates over this and weight down with a clean stone or jars filled with sand. Let stand in a warm place for three or four weeks until it ferments. After forty-eight hours if a brine has not formed, add a little salt water (suitable to taste) to cover the cabbage. After two days more, add more salt water, if necessary, until brine forms over the board cover and a scum appears. Remove the cloth cover, taking the scum with it; rinse thoroughly in cold water, wring dry and return to its place. Continue to do this every few days until it ceases to ferment. This will require four or five weeks. It is then ready to use and may be stored in any cool, dark place. To keep what is left of sauerkraut after winter use through the summer, squeeze out the brine through a cheesecloth. Select an earthenware jar, sprinkle the bottom with salt and pack the sauerkraut in this. Make a brine by dissolving one tablespoon of salt to a quart of cold water. Bring to a boil over a slow fire, removing the scum as it rises. Set aside to cool and pour over the sauerkraut. Lay over the top several thicknesses of cheesecloth and tie over the jar a piece of cotton batting. This will keep until the hottest days of summer.

PUTTING UP ON THE TRAIL

DRYING FRUITS

Tips for successful fruit drying: Avoid overripe, blemished or bruised fruits. Slice pieces thinly. Spread the pieces without touching each other so sun and air can do the job well and quickly. Use a solution of 1 tablespoon ascorbic acid to 1 quart of water **or** use $1/4$ teaspoon sodium bisulfite to 1 quart water to prevent excessive browning. Do not keep fruit in holding solution for more than one hour. **Amounts to use:** 25 pounds of fresh picked fruit such as apples, apricots, peaches or pears will yield 4-8 pounds of dried fruit, depending on the fruit and the weight loss from peelings, pits, seeds or cores. **Berries:** Blackberries, boysenberries, huckleberries and raspberries are not recommended for drying because of their high seed content and slow drying rate. However, they do make excellent fruit leather. **Storing Dried Fruit:** Moisture, air and light must be eliminated for successful fruit storage. Store small quantities in airtight containers. Keep in a dry, dark, cool place.

PEACH LEATHER

When sugar was available, "leathers" were a favorite way of preserving peaches and other fruits.

Measure one-half cupful of sugar for each pound of peeled, stoned peaches. Put fruit and sugar into a preserving kettle; bring slowly to a boil and simmer until most of the moisture has cooked away, mashing to a smooth paste as they cook. Oil a large platter; cover with a piece of muslin and spread the cooked peaches on it in a thin layer. Put the paste in the sun until thoroughly dry, then roll it in the cloth and store in a cool, dry place. To eat, unroll and tear off pieces.

PUTTING UP ON THE TRAIL

SUN-DRIED FRUITS AND VEGETABLES

Pare and slice apples, apricots, peaches, pears, carrots, zucchini, celery, etc. Using a large blunt-nosed needle and heavy thread, pierce and string each piece of fruit or vegetable, leaving space for air to circulate between pieces. Hang out to dry in a partially sunny spot (direct sunlight may cause apricots to become bitter) or hang the strings across an open window that gets some sun. Fruits and vegetables dried this way will keep for months in an airtight container.

PUMPKIN

Slice the pumpkin around in circles, take the seeds out, peel it and hang it on a stick crosswise of the joists of the house. Let it hang there until it dries. Then store it in sacks. Cook it several hours and then season it with hog meat and grease.

SWEET POTATOES

Boil the potatoes until done. Slip off the skins and slice. Put on a clean, white cloth and put out in the sun each day. Then stack for winter use in pudding, pie, etc. or just peel and slice without boiling and set out to dry.

CORN

Corn was cut as if it were going to be cooked, twice around the cob, and then spread out in the sun, sometimes in a piece of tin.

PUTTING UP ON THE TRAIL

OKRA

Slice okra. Put on a piece of metal which has been covered with brown paper or on a white cloth to keep the okra off the metal or tin sheet being used. Place thinly on the sheet and put out in the sun. Cover at night. Let dry until ready to take off the paper. Remove and put in cloth bag until desired to use for cooking.

APPLES

Wash, peel and core apples; slice very thin. Place in a single layer on wire screen or white cloth and place in sun to dry. Take in at night. Apples will dry in 3-4 days of sunshine. When dry, place in bags until ready to use. **Note:** Winesap and Wolf River are good varieties to use.

LEATHERBRITCHES BEANS

Wash and drain a batch of firm green beans. Remove ends and strings. Use large darning needle with heavy white thread and pierce the pod near the middle of each, pushing them along the thread so that they are about 1/4 inch apart. Hang up the strings of beans in a warm, well ventilated place to dry. They will shrivel and turn greenish gray. To cook in the winter time, as the pioneers did, cover with water and soak overnight. Drain, renew water and parboil slowly for 1/2 hour. Drain again. Cook slowly with ham hock or salt pork until tender.

DRYING HERBS

Cut on a bright day just before they blossom. Tie in bunches; label and hang in dry, airy, dustless place to dry quickly as possible. When leaves are dry enough to crumble, strip from branches and place in fruit jars. Cover and label jars. Watch for a few days and if moisture forms on glass, remove leaves and dry longer (they must be thoroughly dry).

PUTTING UP ON THE TRAIL

TO KEEP CORN FOR THE WINTER

When boiled, cut the corn off the cob and spread it on dishes; set these in the oven to dry. If you have no oven it can be dried in a stove of moderate heat or round a fire. When perfectly dry, tie it up in muslin bags and hang them in a dry place. When you use it, boil it until soft in water; mix flour, milk, butter, pepper and salt together and stir in.

TOMAHAWK HOMINY

The pioneer used wood ashes to make hominy, a trick they learned from the Indians. Hominy was served with butter or gravy. Some cooks fried hominy in a skillet with bacon drippings. Hominy was frequently served as a cereal or as a vegetable.

Remove husks; wash and shell the field corn to equal 1 quart. Add 2 quarts of cold water and 2 tablespoons of baking soda; soak overnight. In the morning, bring the corn and the soaking liquid to a boil in a kettle. Cook for 3 hours or until the hulls loosen. Add more water, if necessary. Drain off the water; wash corn in cold water, rubbing vigorously until the hulls are removed. Bring the corn to a boil again with 2 quarts of cold water; drain. Repeat the boiling step with fresh water; drain and add salt.

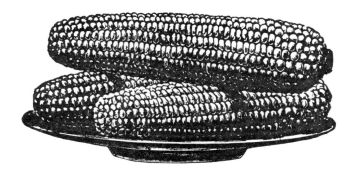

PUTTING UP ON THE TRAIL

MAKING JERKY

Cut meat into strips about an inch thick and hang it in the sun, where in a few days it will dry so well that it may be packed in sacks and transported over long journeys. When there is not time to jerk the meat by the slow process described, it may be done in a few hours by building an open framework of small sticks about two feet above the ground, placing the strips of meat upon the top of it and keeping a slow fire beneath, which dries the meat rapidly. The jerking process may be done upon the march without any loss of time by stretching lines from front to rear upon the outside of loaded wagons and suspending the meat upon them, where it is allowed to remain until sufficiently cured to be packed away. Salt is never used in this process and is not required, as the meat, if kept dry, rarely putrefies. If travelers have ample transportation, it will be a wise precaution, in passing through the buffalo range, to lay in a supply of jerked meat for the future.

SALT PORK

This is similar to bacon except for the way it is cured. Salt pork is soaked in a barrel of strong salt water for 10 days to 2 weeks, then placed in boxes with a layer of salt, then pork, alternating salt and pork until the box is filled. When salt pork is cooked, slice same as bacon, but first parboil it in a pan of boiling water to remove the excess salt. Fry the same as bacon.

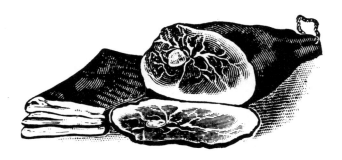

PUTTING UP ON THE TRAIL

TO SMOKE BACON

Take a tin pan or kettle of corn cobs and set them on the fire so as to make them smoke; then turn bottom side up over the smoking cobs the barrel or whatever you wish to pickle or salt your bacon in, so as to thoroughly smoke the inside of it. Burn at least two pans of cobs under it, so as to smoke it well. Then pack the hams, shoulders or other meat that you wish to make bacon of, in the cask, and after preparing your pickle, heat it nearly boiling hot and pour it on the meat and let the meat stay until it is made into bacon, ready for use and well smoked. The bacon can remain in the pickle until used and you can watch the pickle in the summer and should it ferment, scald it over.

CAMP SITE CURED MEATS-BRINED MEAT, CORNED BEEF

Rub meat well with salt and drain overnight to draw out blood. Make a brine as follows: For 100 pounds of meat, use 8 pounds salt, 2 pounds brown sugar, 2 ounces saltpeter, 4 gallons of boiling water. Dissolve all ingredients well in boiling water and cool. Pack meat in jars or barrel and cover with cold brine. The amount of salt varies a little for sugar cured ham and bacon. If meat is to be cured in warm weather, more salt should be used. Nine or ten pounds of salt might be safer in this case. If a mild cure is preferred and the meat is not to be kept very long, less salt or 8 pounds is recommended as in recipe above. Bacon strips should remain in the brine from 4-6 weeks. If the brine becomes ropy, take out all the meat and place in the brine again. Be sure that the brine covers the meat and that the meat is weighted down. In about 10 days it is a good plan to move the pieces about in the container, taking off brine if necessary. This seems to give a little more even cure if done several times. Elk, venison and beef are all good cured in this brine. **Note:** If pork is cured, it then may be taken out and smoked in a smoke house. Use ash or apple wood to make a heavy, dense smoke. Mutton may be used, also.

PUTTING UP ON THE TRAIL

PICKLED PIGS' FEET

Scrape and clean the pigs' feet thoroughly. Put in kettle and boil for four or five hours until soft. Add salt to taste during boiling. Take out and pack in a crock or stone jar. Boil vinegar and spice it well; pour over pigs' feet until covered. Allow them to stand for several days before serving. To serve, split them, make a batter of two eggs, a cup of milk, salt, a teaspoonful of butter, with flour enough to make a thick batter. Dip each piece in this and fry in hot lard or dip them in beaten egg and flour and fry. Good eaten cold or warm.

PIONEER PICKLED BEEF TONGUE

Makes approximately 3 pounds beef tongue. Boil tongue approximately 4 hours or until tender. When cool, the rough may be removed with a sharp knife. Slice and soak in cold water for one hour. Skin when cooked. Mix in saucepan:

2 c. water
2 c. vinegar
1 rounded T. vinegar
2 T. pickling spice
1 tsp. salt

Bring to boil. Pour over drained beef tongue. One large onion may be sliced and added.

It is not yet eight o'clock when the first watch is to be set; the evening meal is just over. Near the river a violin makes lively music, and some youths improvise a dance; in another quarter a flute whispers its lament to the deepening night. It has been a prosperous day; more than 20 miles have been accomplished.
- Jesse Applegate, 1843

CHRISTMAS MINCEMEAT

1/2 c. finely chopped suet
1/2 c. washed, scraped & grated carrots
6 lg. eating apples, washed, peeled, cored & chopped
2 c. seeded raisins or currants, soaked & drained
1/2 c. ground leftover cooked beef or cooked hamburger
1/2 c. finely cut citron
1/2 c. finely cut candied orange peel
2 T. powdered cinnamon
1/2 T. grated nutmeg
1/2 T. powdered cloves
1 1/2 c. light molasses or 1 c. brown sugar & 1/2 c. water
2 c. boiled cider

Mix all together in agate or enamel kettle; bring to boiling and boil 5 minutes. Pack at once into hot sterile glass jars and seal. Set in cool place 10 days to ripen. Makes 6 pints.

TO MAKE LARD

Take the leaf fat from the inside of a bacon hog, cut it small and put it in an iron kettle, which must be perfectly free from any musty taste; set it over a steady moderate fire until nothing but scraps remain of the meat; the heat must be kept up, but gentle, that it may not burn the lard; spread a coarse cloth in a wire sieve and strain the liquid into tin basins which will hold two or three quarts; squeeze out all the fat from the scraps. When the lard in the pans is cold, press a piece of muslin close upon it, trim it off the edge of the pan and keep it in a cool place. Or, it may be kept in wooden kegs with close covers. Lard made with one-third as much beef suet as fat, is supposed by many persons to keep better.

PUTTING UP ON THE TRAIL

KEEPING EGGS FRESH

All it is necessary to do to keep eggs through summer is to procure small, clean wooden or tin vessels, holding from ten to twenty gallons, and a barrel, more or less, of common, fine ground land plaster or cornmeal. Begin by putting on the bottom of the vessel two or three inches of plaster/meal and then, having fresh eggs, with the yolks unbroken, set them up, small end down, close to each other, but not crowding, and make the first layer. Then add more plaster and enough so the eggs will stand upright and set up the second layer; then another deposit of plaster/meal. Eggs so packed and subjected to a temperature of at least 85 degrees, if not 90 degrees, during August and September, come out fresh and if one could be certain of not having a temperature of more than 75 degrees to contend with, eggs could be kept by these means all the year round. Observe that the eggs must be fresh laid, the yolks unbroken, the packing done in small vessels and with clean, fine ground land plaster or cornmeal and care must be taken that no egg so presses on another as to break the shell. Eggs may be kept good for a year in the following manner: To a pail of water, put of unslacked lime and coarse salt each a pint; keep it in a cellar or cool place and put the eggs in, as fresh laid as possible. It is well to keep a stone pot of this lime water ready.

Another method is to make a solution of borax (a heaping teaspoonful of pulverized borax to a pint of boiling water); let stand until the solution becomes warm, but do not allow it to so cool that the borax will crystallize; dip the eggs quickly then. Keep in a cool place; the borax will crystallize around the egg, therefore keep out the air and preserve the egg. Eggs were kept in a number of different ways; by coating with paraffin, storing in brine, packing in barrels of sawdust stored in a cool place, or preserving in borax. The point of all these methods was to provide an airtight seal.

DUTCH OVEN COOKING

Home cooking at its best, over the chips, on the prairie.

FORT LARAMIE

The structure shown in the picture (front side of this divider) was originally built in 1841 and was known as Fort John. The U.S. Army purchased the fort in 1848 and renamed it Fort Laramie. Travelers used the fort as a focal point on the Oregon Trail until the 1890's.

In the early days of the Oregon Trail, Fort Laramie was not a military post, but a trapper's trading post. The pioneers strolled across the fort grounds to the trader's store and bought such items as coffee, pepsin compound and pickles. Travelers often rested and socialized for a day or two at this significant Oregon Trail post.

DUTCH OVEN COOKING

Cooking over an open fire might be fun on a weekend camping trip, but for the pioneers, preparing edible meals over a cookfire was an everyday necessity. On the trail, cooking equipment was limited to only the essentials. One of the most useful pieces of cookware was the Dutch oven. These large, round, cast iron pots allowed the pioneers to roast meat, cook stews, or prepare foods normally baked in an oven at home.

The Dutch oven was placed directly on the hot coals for preheating and cooking. After it was preheated, the food was poured in and the lid placed on top. Coals were then arranged on top of the lid to provide even baking from both directions.

The first part of this section includes recipes using ingredients that the pioneers may have very likely used on the trail. There are also modern Dutch oven recipes that can be easily prepared at home or while camping.❖

DUTCH OVEN COOKING

"OLD TIME" DUTCH OVEN COOKING

PRAIRIE FIRE RABBIT

2 rabbits, cut into serving chunks
Salt
1 c. flour
Pepper

Put rabbit in boiling water. Simmer 20 minutes. Drain. Dry mix flour, salt and pepper. Roll rabbit in flour; fry in hot lard. If you would like gravy, drain most of lard off after all frying is done. Save about 3 tablespoons. Pour in 1 cup of buttermilk and simmer, do not boil, scraping the bottom of the Dutch oven.

WILD YOUNG RABBIT

1 rabbit, cut in pieces
1/2 c. flour
1/4 c. butter or margarine
2 c. milk
Salt & pepper to taste

Marinade solution:

1/4 c. salt
1/4 c. vinegar
Water

Before cooking, wild rabbit should be washed overnight in salt, vinegar and water. Remove rabbit from the marinade. Dry. Season with salt and pepper. Roll in flour. Fry in a Dutch oven in plenty of butter or margarine over a low heat. Turn several times until evenly browned. Cover and cook slowly until tender. Turn pieces during this process. When done, remove to a hot platter. Pour off all but about 1/4 cup of the fat. Blend in 3 tablespoons flour. Slowly add 2 cups milk, stirring to keep smooth. Cook until thickened. Add salt and pepper to taste. Serve with rabbit.

DUTCH OVEN COOKING

KETTLE-FRIED RABBIT

2 sm. rabbits, cut up
2 eggs, beaten
3 c. milk
1 1/4 c. flour
1/2 tsp. salt
2 T. baking powder
1 qt. water
1 T. salt

Soak rabbit overnight in salt water (1 quart water to 1 tablespoon salt). Drain. Mix well the egg, milk, flour, salt and baking powder. Dip rabbit in batter and deep fry in hot lard. Meat should be tender and golden brown.

DUTCH OVEN COOKING

RIFLE RABBIT RAGOUT

1 1/2 lbs. rabbit meat
1/2 c. flour
1 tsp. salt
1/2 tsp. pepper
3 T. fat
4 potatoes, diced
4 carrots, sliced
2 onions, diced
Flour
Water

Cut rabbit into 1-inch cubes. Mix flour, salt and pepper together and dust meat with mixture. Melt fat in large kettle; add meat and brown. Add enough hot water to cover meat; cover kettle and simmer 2 hours or until meat is tender. Add vegetables and cook an additional half hour. Thicken stew with 1 1/2 tablespoons flour and water. Once gravy is thick enough, drop in dumpling batter by spoonfuls to make dumplings (below). Cover kettle tightly and boil gently for 15 minutes. Serve gravy, meat and vegetables. Serves 3-4.

Dumplings:

1 c. sifted flour
2 tsp. baking powder
1/2 tsp. salt
1 egg
1/2 c. milk

Mix and sift the dry ingredients together. Beat egg; add milk and finally add the flour mixture. Mix lightly.

BUTTERMILK DEER STEAK

Buttermilk
Salt & pepper to taste
Tenderized deer steak

Soak tenderized steak in buttermilk for 2-3 hours. Dip in flour and fry in hot oil until done.

DUTCH OVEN COOKING

ASH HOLLOW DEER STEAK

Deer steak
Salt & pepper to taste
Flour
Lard for frying

Cut all of white membrane from deer steak. Beat with a mallet to tenderize. Lightly salt and heavily pepper steak on both sides. Coat with flour and fry in hot oil. Let get done on one side before turning. Do not turn again.

PLATTE RIVER FRIED CATFISH

2 lbs. fresh catfish (pan dressed or fillets)
1 1/2 c. cornmeal
1/4 tsp. pepper
2 tsp. salt
2 eggs, beaten
2 tsp. milk
Lard for frying

Season fish with salt and pepper. Combine eggs and milk. Dip fish into egg mixture, then roll in cornmeal to coat. Fill frying pan 1/2 full with oil. Fry for 7-8 minutes or until first side is golden brown. Turn and cook 7-8 minutes more or until fish browns and flakes easily with fork. Fish may be placed in a warm oven to keep crisp for serving.

There we were, more than two thousand miles from home. . . Go ahead we must, no matter what we were to encounter.
- Ezra Meek, 1852, Oregon

DUTCH OVEN COOKING

CAMPFIRE TROUT

Sm. trout
1/2 tsp. butter
Salt
Pepper

Remove entrails and gills from a small trout and wash fish thoroughly in fresh water. Place butter inside rib cage and salt and pepper entire fish to taste. Place trout on grill over campfire coals and turn occasionally. Usually takes about an hour to cook the fish.

COLUMBIA RIVER TROUT

1 lg. trout
Salt
Pepper
Cornmeal
Melted butter

Cut cleaned fish to lie flat when open. Coat fish with cornmeal. Brush generously with butter. Cook in hot skillet, allowing 6-8 minutes per side for a 4 to 5-pound trout.

ROAST DUCK, VENISON OR RABBIT

About 1 1/2 c. vinegar
2 lg. onions, sliced
2 tsp. salt & pepper
1 bay leaf
Raw bacon

Make punctures in meat and stuff with little pieces of bacon. Marinate meat or fowl overnight, if possible, with the vinegar, onions, bay leaf, salt and pepper. Heat oil in roasting pan and brown meat on all sides. Add water, as necessary (1 cup at a time); cook until tender.

DUTCH OVEN COOKING

PIONEER'S DELIGHT STEW

1-1 ½ lbs. stew meat, cubed
½-¾ c. chopped onion to taste
2 or 3 carrots (opt.)
7 or 8 potatoes, depending on size & number of servings

Brown meat in Dutch oven until nearly done, adding 2 or 3 cups water and onions, salt and pepper to taste. Let come to a boil, reduce heat and let simmer 20-30 minutes or until meat is tender, adding water as needed. Peel carrots and cut crosswise, let cook approximately 10 minutes before adding potatoes. The potatoes can be peeled and cut into 1-inch cubes and added. Cover with water and let cook 20-30 minutes, after it comes to a boil again or until the potatoes and carrots are done. Serves 6-8.

LIGHTNING BOLT STEW

Leftover meat was often used for stew. Add extra potatoes, carrots and whole onions to the leftover meat and cooking broth. Cook for quite a long time until the stew is thickened and very tender.

ALCOVE SPRINGS SQUIRREL STEW

Cut the squirrel into six or eight pieces; cook in a vessel with a tight lid and just enough water to cover. Add salt and pepper to suit the taste. Add 1 tablespoon of pure lard. Cover and cook for a long time until quite tender. Serve with hot biscuits or dumplings.

DUTCH OVEN COOKING

McLOUGHLIN'S FRIED COON

1 dressed coon
1 c. cooking oil
1 tsp. vinegar
1 c. cornmeal
1 onion, sliced
Water to cover

Cut the coon into serving portions and parboil for 1 hour or until tender with the onion, water and vinegar. Roll the coon portions in the cornmeal and fry in a large skillet with the oil until golden brown. Some folks put ½ cup flour in with the cornmeal.

BEAR CROSSING STEW

2 lbs. bear meat
Lard or bacon drippings
2 T. flour
¼ tsp. black pepper
1 tsp. salt
10 juniper berries
1 ½ pts. water
8 med. potatoes
Few mushrooms

Cube bear meat and dice potatoes. Cook bear meat and lard in small Dutch oven until done. Add flour, black pepper and salt. When all juices and oil are absorbed in flour, add juniper berries, water, potatoes and mushrooms. Simmer in closed Dutch oven for 30 minutes.

DUTCH OVEN COOKING

MISSOURI RIVER TURTLE

1 lb. turtle meat, cubed
1 tsp. salt
1/4 c. lard
1/2 c. flour
1 tsp. black pepper

Parboil meat for 1/2 hour, then drain and sprinkle with salt and pepper. Roll in flour. Now fry the meat in lard over medium heat until tender and brown on all sides.

LONE PINE POTTED PIGEONS

4 pigeons
1 slice fat salt pork
Salt & pepper
2 level T. butter
2 level T. flour

Clean and truss the birds as for roasting. Cut the pork into small pieces, cut out the fat and brown the birds in it. Put them in a casserole or baking dish. Add the seasoning and stock; cover closely and cook about two hours. Remove the pigeons to the serving dish and thicken the gravy with the butter and flour rubbed smoothly together. Pour the gravy over the birds.

DEVIL'S GATE FRIED QUAIL

Clean and wash quail. Dry. Salt and pepper and dredge with flour. Heat a heavy Dutch oven with close fitting lid containing about 3/4 cup oil. Fry quail until golden brown on all sides. Cover and let simmer until tender. Serve on hot platter. Delicious with home-made hot biscuits.

DUTCH OVEN COOKING

WYETH'S BAKED DOVES

Doves
Salt & pepper to taste
Flour
Butter or oleo

Generously salt and pepper doves. Dust with flour. Melt butter or oleo in skillet and brown doves on both sides. Remove doves to baking dish. Add water to pan drippings and pour over doves. Cover tightly and bake in slow oven.

CAMPFIRE STEW

3 lbs. beef or venison, cubed
1/2 c. flour
1/2 lb. bacon
1 tsp. thyme
2 med. onions, diced
1 lb. carrots
2 1/2 lbs. potatoes
1/4 c. vinegar
2 c. water

Fry bacon in Dutch oven. Flour beef and brown with bacon. Add onions; stir and cook 5 minutes. Add all other ingredients and bring to boil. Remove from heat; cover and cover lid with coals. Cook, stirring occasionally, for 1-1 1/2 hours. **Modern version:** Add four 8-ounce cans tomato sauce.

I have a great desire to see Oregon. . .the beautiful scenery of plain and mountains, and. . .the wild animals and natural curiosities in abundance.
- Elizabeth Wood, 1851

DUTCH OVEN COOKING

DUTCH OVEN VEGETABLES

8-10 potatoes, peeled & sliced
5-6 carrots, sliced
1 lb. bacon, cut up
2 onions, chopped

Partially fry bacon in Dutch oven. Add onions, carrots and potatoes. Mix well. Bake with lid, covered with coals (no bottom heat) for 45-50 minutes.

MT. HOOD POTATOES

1/4 c. bacon fat or butter
4 c. thinly sliced raw potatoes
1 med. onion, thinly sliced
1 tsp. salt
1/8 tsp. black pepper
1/2 tsp. leaf sage

Heat bacon fat in iron skillet, or Dutch oven, over low heat; add potatoes, onion and seasonings. Cover and cook about 15 minutes. Turn potatoes and cover. Continue cooking 15 more minutes or until potatoes are tender.

WAGON SPOKE TURNIPS

Wash and peel several small or medium-sized turnips. Slice them in 1/4-inch slices. Place into a stew pan in a small amount of water. Boil until tender. Season with about 2 tablespoons of butter or bacon grease, about 1 teaspoon of sugar and pepper and salt to taste.

DUTCH OVEN COOKING

GREAT MIGRATION TURNIPS

Wash and peel 8-10 medium-sized turnips. Cut in slices; cover and cook in a small amount of boiling water until tender, about 20 minutes. When turnips are tender, drain thoroughly. Add 1 teaspoon of sugar, butter or bacon grease the size of walnut. Add a dash of pepper. Mash and serve hot.

WILTED DANDELION GREENS

2 qts. dandelion greens
4 T. bacon fat
1/4 c. mild vinegar
1 tsp. salt

Wash the greens thoroughly. Cut into small pieces with scissors. Heat the bacon fat, vinegar and salt in a skillet. Add the greens; cover and cook at moderate heat until the greens are wilted. Serve at once.

SASSAFRAS TEA

4 c. water
6 pieces of sassafras root, 4 inches long or 1 c. of chips
1/2 c. honey, raw is best

Rinse the roots with water until all the dirt is off. Place into a pot. Pour the water over the roots and bring to a boil. After reaching a boil, turn down the heat, letting the tea steam. Add honey and let it cook for 30 minutes. Then serve. (Roots must be dried before using.)

DUTCH OVEN COOKING

NATURE'S VEGETABLE SOUP

Put six quarts of water to boil in a large pot with a quarter of a pound of suet or two ounces of drippings; season it with a level tablespoonful of salt, half a teaspoonful of pepper and a few sprigs of parsley and dried herbs. While it is boiling, prepare cabbage, turnips, beans or any vegetables in season; throw them into the boiling soup and when they have boiled up thoroughly, set the pot at the side of the fire, where it will simmer for about two hours. Then take up some of the vegetables without breaking and use them with any gravy you may have on hand or with a quarter of a pound of bacon, sliced and fried, for the bulk of the meal. The soup, after being seasoned to taste, can be eaten with bread.

EASY SUNUP BREAKFAST

1 potato per person plus 5 for the pot
1 lb. bacon, cut in 1-inch pieces
1 onion, diced
Eggs
Salt & pepper

Fry bacon in oven. Add onion. Saute. Dice potatoes into ¼-inch cubes and fry in oven until tender and brown. Crack eggs over top of mixture, 2 per person. Remove from heat. Cover and cover lid with coals. Bake 5-7 minutes or until eggs are cooked to your liking. Season and serve.

DUTCH OVEN COOKING

CORN PONE

1 1/2 c. yellow cornmeal
1/2 c. white flour
2 tsp. baking powder
1 tsp. salt
1 c. milk
1 egg, beaten
3 T. melted bacon fat

Mix the dry ingredients. Add the milk and the beaten egg and stir to make the mixture uniform. Stir in the bacon fat. Heat a slightly greased skillet and drop the batter onto the surface, spreading it out with a kitchen spoon. When one side is brown, turn and brown the other side. Both sides should brown in 2 1/2-3 minutes.

SUNDOWN SOURDOUGH BISCUITS

1/2 c. starter
1 c. milk
2 1/2 c. flour
1 tsp. baking powder
1 T. sugar
1/2 tsp. salt
1/2 tsp. soda
Butter or margarine, melted

Mix starter, milk and 1 cup flour the night before. Pour out onto 1 cup of flour. Combine 1/2 cup flour, soda, baking powder, sugar and salt. Pour over dough. Mix well and begin to knead lightly. Roll out to 1/2 inch thick. Cut out and dip into melted butter. Let rise 1/2 hour. Bake about 30-40 minutes or until brown. Use 10 coals on the bottom and 18 on top.

DUTCH OVEN COOKING

SIOUX JELLIED SNAKE

1 med. snake
2 c. Indian vinegar
1 handful mint
2 fingers coltsfoot salt

(Any fat snake will do for this recipe, but rattlesnake is best.) Cut off head and skin and take out intestines. Cut into 1-inch pieces. Wash in cold water. Put vinegar, mint and salt in the same container. Put the pieces of snake on top and cover with cold water. Let stand overnight. Put container on hot burner in morning and simmer slowly for about 35 minutes. Remove from heat and let cool. Ready to eat when jelly has set.

SANDHILLS FRIED RATTLER

Rattlesnake
Salt
1 tsp. vinegar
Flour

Skin and cut into 3-inch pieces. Soak in salt water for 1 hour. Change water; add 1 teaspoon vinegar to water. Soak for 1 hour. Drain and dry on paper towels. Roll in flour and fry.

DUTCH OVEN COOKING

VELVET TAIL RATTLESNAKE

The snakes should be kept alive and in good condition until they are eaten. Never bludgeon them with clubs or rocks; the heads should be removed with an ax and disposed of immediately. Then split the body down the belly and remove skin. You should then gut and clean in fresh water. Due to reflex action, the snake will squirm and wiggle for some time after the head is removed and may crawl out of the pan if left unattended. Dice the snake in about 2-inch pieces using a sharp knife. Soak these pieces overnight. There are two good ways to prepare: (1.) 1 egg, cup milk and 1 teaspoon salt. Make a batter similar to batter for fried chicken; roll the pieces in the batter and then in equal parts of cracker crumbs and flour. Deep fat fry until golden brown. (2.) Fix same as above but instead of deep frying, pan fry and then simmer in 1 cup of water until tender, as you would Southern fried chicken.

MODERN DUTCH OVEN COOKING

OLD-TIME BEEF BRISKET

3-3 1/2 lbs. fresh boneless beef brisket
6 med. carrots
2 med. onions, halved
4 lg. potatoes, diced
2 celery stalks, cut into chunks
1 T. salt
1/4 tsp. pepper
10 whole cloves

Place brisket in Dutch oven. Add vegetables, except potatoes, seasonings and barely cover with water. Simmer, covered, do not boil, until fork tender, 3-4 hours. Transfer meat and vegetables to hot platter and keep hot while cooking potatoes in broth or dumplings using biscuit mix. Thicken broth for gravy. Slice brisket across grain, slanting knife slightly.

DUTCH OVEN COOKING

CORNED BEEF AND CABBAGE

4-5 c. cabbage, shredded
1 (11-oz.) can cream of celery soup
1 tsp. onion, minced
1 (12-oz.) can corned beef

Mix cabbage, soup and onions; place in Dutch oven. Slice or chop corned beef and place on top of cabbage. Bake about 20 minutes or until cabbage is done. Serves 4-6.

OX BOW BEEF RIBS

3 T. cooking oil
3 lbs. beef short ribs or at least 1 rib per person
3 T. molasses
2 T. vinegar
1 c. celery, chopped
1 c. green peas
1 (8-oz.) can tomato paste
1 can beef broth
1/2 tsp. dried thyme

Heat the cooking oil in Dutch oven and brown the ribs on all sides. Add the other ingredients and bake for 2 hours or until the meat is tender. Occasionally check for adequate liquid. Add small amount of water, if needed. Remove the liquid fat with a spoon. After serving the ribs, the vegetables and broth may be served over the ribs. Serves 8.

Once or twice in midstream, the wheels sunk into the yielding sands so threateningly that we half believed we had dreaded and avoided the sea all our lives to be shipwrecked in a 'mud wagon' in the middle of the desert at last.
- Mark Twain, Roughing It

DUTCH OVEN COOKING

DUSTY TRAIL DINNER

2 lbs. ground beef
6 lbs. potatoes
1 pkg. carrots
6 onions
1 pkg. onion soup mix

Mix onion soup mix in ground beef and form large, thick patties. Peel and quarter potatoes, carrots and onions. Place beef patties with vegetables into preheated, Pam sprayed Dutch oven. Cook over coals, turning frequently and setting off and on the coals until cooked thoroughly. **Variation:** Turnips, parsnips, etc. may be added for variety. Also, if you don't have a Dutch oven, wrap patties individually with some of the vegetables in foil and cook on open barbecue.

2,000 MILE SWISS STEAK

1 (3-lb.) round steak, 1 inch thick
3 T. margarine
1 tsp. salt
3 sticks celery, chopped
1/2 c. catsup
1 T. dried parsley flakes
1 lg. onion, chopped

Brown both sides of beef in margarine in Dutch oven. Add other ingredients and cook, covered, for 2 hours. Add small amount of water, if needed, to keep sauce thinner. Serves 8.

DUTCH OVEN COOKING

SWISS STEAK

3 1/2 lbs. of 1 1/2-inch pot roast (round bone type)
Cooking oil
1 lg. can tomatoes
3 Spanish onions
2 fresh cloves garlic
Salt & pepper to taste
3 green peppers, diced
2 tsp. paprika
1 c. sherry

Put oil in Dutch oven and brown the meat, adding the liquid from the tomatoes. Simmer for 10 minutes. Peel and quarter the onions. Add the onions, chopped garlic cloves, diced green peppers, salt and pepper and paprika. Place whole tomatoes on top of meat. Add sherry. Cook with lid on until brown over slow heat, about 2 hours. Serve rice on the side or mashed potatoes. It's a yummy dish!

BEST-EVER BAKED CHICKEN

3 lbs. drumsticks & thighs
1 lemon
2 tsp. garlic salt
1/2 c. flour
1/2 tsp. paprika
1/4 c. butter
1 (14 1/4-oz.) can chicken broth
1/3 c. onion, chopped

Wipe chicken with damp paper towel. Rub with cut lemon. Sprinkle with garlic salt and let stand 10 minutes. Combine flour and paprika in paper bag. Add chicken and shake to coat well. Brown in butter in Dutch oven or electric skillet. Remove chicken from pan when cooking is completed. Add remaining seasoned flour, about 2 tablespoons, and brown slightly, stirring to loosen drippings. Add chicken broth and onion. Cook, stirring until thickened. Return chicken to pan. Cover and bake about 1 hour over moderate heat.

DUTCH OVEN COOKING

TRAIL RIDER'S CHICKEN-N-RICE

2 chickens, skinned & quartered
2 cans cream of mushroom soup
1/4 lb. bacon
1 green pepper, chopped
1 c. celery, chopped
2 c. water
1 c. rice
1 onion, chopped
1 T. salt

Fry bacon in Dutch oven; add rice and brown. Add onions, soup, celery, peppers, salt, water and chicken. Bring to boil. Remove from heat and bake with 6-8 coals bottom, 14-18 coals on lid for 1 hour.

HUNGRY MAN'S COUNTRY RIBS

Enough ribs to fit your Dutch oven

Glaze:

2 T. catsup
2 T. honey

Mix glaze and pour over ribs in Dutch oven. Set oven on coals and place coals on lid. Cook 1 hour.

HAM AND CHEESE CASSEROLE

1 pkg. Kraft macaroni & cheese
1 1/2 c. chopped ham
1 can peas

Cook macaroni in boiling water in Dutch oven. You can do this by placing covered pot in the fire. When macaroni is cooked, drain off water, add milk and cheese packet and butter according to package. Add ham and drained peas. Stir gently. Set on 1 shovelful of coals for 10 minutes. Serves 3.

DUTCH OVEN COOKING

FORT LARAMIE PORK CHOPS

8 pork chops
6 med. potatoes, thick sliced
2 med. onions, quartered
2 c. cracker crumbs or Shake 'N Bake seasoned to taste with
    salt, pepper & garlic powder

Use a 14-inch Dutch oven preheated with ¼ inch of pure olive oil. Coat pork chops with crumbs and brown on each side. Move pork chops to one side of the Dutch oven and stack, if necessary. Place potatoes and onions in remaining side of oven; cover and cook about 45 minutes with less coals on the bottom and more coals on the lid. Check meat after the first 15-20 minutes for burning while turning meat and potatoes and adjusting the amount of coals as necessary. Turn lid and oven periodically about ¼ turn in opposite directions to prevent burning of food on top and bottom. **Variation:** Chicken breasts may be cooked in the same manner as above.

SCOTTS BLUFF SAUERKRAUT & PORK HOCKS

4-5 lbs. smoked pork hocks
4-5 c. water
1 onion, sliced
½ tsp. marjoram or leaves
2 lbs. sauerkraut, drained
½ tsp. celery seed (opt.)

Place meat, water, onion and marjoram in Dutch oven. Heat to boiling. Reduce heat; cover tightly and simmer 1 hour or more. Remove oven from heat. Drain liquid, being sure to reserve 1 cup. Add sauerkraut, celery seed and reserved liquid to meat. Cover and simmer 30 more minutes.

DUTCH OVEN COOKING

MOUNTAIN MAN BARBECUE RIBS

2 lbs. pork ribs, cut into serving pieces
1 onion, diced
1 c. water
2 c. barbecue sauce
Garlic salt to taste
Pepper to taste

Spray Dutch oven with Pam. Preheat Dutch oven over hot coals, including lid, for a few minutes. Place ribs sprinkled with garlic salt and pepper in Dutch oven with 1 cup water. Place on coals until boiling. Reduce heat by turning and removing some coals, allowing to cook slowly for 1 hour. Remove and drain off liquid. Pour barbecue sauce over ribs, making sure all ribs are covered with sauce. Continue cooking, turning Dutch oven and lid, with hot coals, for approximately $1/2$ hour more.

HOMESTEAD HAM AND POTATOES

8-10 potatoes, peeled & cubed
2 lbs. ham, cubed
2 onions, diced
2 c. milk
3-4 c. cheese, shredded
$1/4$ lb. bacon

Fry bacon in Dutch oven, stirring to coat sides. Add onions, then ham and potatoes. Stir well. Add the milk; cover and bake 40-50 minutes. Top with cheese. Cover and bake until potatoes are done and cheese is melted.

DUTCH OVEN COOKING

WESTWARD HO PORK CHOPS

8 pork chops
2 T. cooking oil
1 can mushroom soup
1 tsp. salt

Brown pork chops in oil. Add soup and salt; cook for 60 minutes in covered Dutch oven. Serves 8. **Variations:** Add 1 can tomato soup. Add 1 tablespoon dried parsley flakes.

CANVAS CHEESY BRAT STEW

6 bratwurst links, cut in $1/2$-inch pieces
4 med. potatoes, cubed
1 (15-oz.) can green beans, drained
1 sm. onion, chopped
1 c. cheddar cheese, grated
1 can cream of mushroom soup
1 c. water

Combine ingredients in Dutch oven. Cover and cook about 45 minutes or until potatoes are done. Serves 4-6.

HIGHWATER FISH

4 T. margarine
4 fillets
2 T. lemon juice
$1/4$ c. milk or sour cream
Parsley

Add oil in Dutch oven; place the lemon juice and milk in, then place the fillets. Bake in oven for 15-20 minutes. Check to be certain fish is done. Serve with parsley sprinkled on fillets. Serves 4.

DUTCH OVEN COOKING

BRAISED FISH

4 T. margarine
8 fillets
Dill weed

Melt 2 tablespoons of margarine in Dutch oven. Place one or two fillets in oven. When fillet is brown, about 6-8 minutes, turn it to brown other side until done. Sprinkle dill weed on top and serve warm. Add more margarine, if needed, for other fillets. Serves 8.

BUFFALO CHIP COON ROAST

1 dressed coon
2 1/2 T. salt
3 carrots, sliced
2 onions, sliced
1 T. black pepper
5 potatoes, quartered

Parboil the coon in a kettle together with the onions, carrots, salt, pepper and just enough water to cover it for 3 1/2 hours; then drain. Next, place the coon in a roaster pan and add potatoes; pour 1 cup the kettle liquid over coon. Cook, covered, for 2 hours at medium temperature, then uncover for 1/2 hour, basting occasionally; then serve.

DUTCH OVEN COOKING

BIG GAME ROAST

(Deer, Elk, Antelope, or Bear Meat)

Marinade mixture:

4 c. cold water
1/2 c. vinegar or wine
1 c. tomato juice
1/4 c. sugar
2 bay leaves
1/2 lemon, sliced
2 carrots
Several stalks celery
2 cloves garlic, chopped
1 T. tenderizer
Salt
Pepper

Wash meat in water several times. Take off all fat you can; clean off all blood you can. Place in roaster with cover, deep enough to bring marinade mixture to top of roast. Mix marinade mixture together; put on meat, then place the pan in refrigerator overnight. The next day, place roaster in oven at 350°. Keep covered. If the roast is from an old buck, it will take from 4 1/2-5 hours. If a young animal, it will cook in less than 3 hours. If liquid evaporates, add water and baste with juice occasionally. At no time allow it to become dry or burn. When done, remove the roast from pan. Strain the juice and mash the vegetables through a strainer. Set aside; skim off fat. Thicken juice for gravy with a little flour and water. **Variations:** You may prefer roasting game meat with buttermilk or adding the flavor of mustard or curry powder. Strips of salt pork placed over the meat not only add to the flavor but help tenderize. Tomatoes, if used, can be either fresh, canned, tomato soup, tomato sauce, tomato paste, puree or juice. Wild meat needs liberal seasoning. Makes 6-8 pounds; 18-24 servings.

DUTCH OVEN COOKING

RANCH-STYLE BEANS

1 (31-oz.) can beans, cooked & drained (navy, pinto or kidney)
1 onion, diced
1 T. molasses or pancake syrup
4 strips bacon, chopped
2 T. brown sugar
1/2 green pepper, diced
1/2 c. ham, diced
1/2 c. barbecue sauce (any kind)

Partially cook bacon, then add rest of ingredients in 8 or 10-inch Dutch oven and simmer on a few coals for 1 hour (4-5 coals below, 8-10 coals on lid). Serve hot from the oven.

INDIAN CORNBREAD

2 c. yellow cornmeal
2 c. Bisquick mix
1/2 c. oil
2 eggs
2 c. milk
1 tsp. salt

Mix dry ingredients well. Combine oil, eggs and milk. Mix with dry ingredients. Pour into 14-inch Dutch oven and bake for 20-30 minutes. Place Dutch oven on coals and add coals to top cover.

DUTCH OVEN COOKING

OLD DUTCH CORNBREAD

2 c. cornmeal
4 c. flour
2 T. baking powder
Milk
1 c. sugar
2 eggs
1 c. lard

Mix dry ingredients thoroughly. Add eggs. Add enough milk to make a medium batter. Bake at 375° for 15-20 minutes or until a toothpick comes out clean when inserted in center. Make sure Dutch oven is well oiled.

SOURDOUGH STARTER

2 c. flour
1 pkg. dry yeast
2 T. sugar
3 c. warm water

In a non-metallic container, mix to a thick batter. Each day for 3 days add 1 cup flour and 3/4 cup warm water; mix well. Feed weekly, if you don't use, or refrigerate and feed monthly. Replace starter used with flour and water. Maintain 2-3 cups starter.

It is on the stroke of seven that the clear notes of the trumpet sound in front; the leading wagons move out of the camp and the rest fall into their places with the precision of clockwork until the spot so full of life sinks back into the solitude that seems to reign over the broad plain and rushing river.

- Jesse Applegate, 1843

DUTCH OVEN COOKING

SOURDOUGH BISCUITS

2 c. flour
1 T. sugar
1 T. baking powder
2-3 T. shortening or butter
3/4 tsp. salt
2 c. sourdough starter (see previous recipe)

Sift flour, sugar, baking powder and salt into large bowl; pour in starter. Mix to a firm dough. Grease 12-inch iron skillet. Pinch off balls the size of walnuts. Place in pan. Set biscuits in warm place 10-15 minutes. Bake in 400° oven for 24-30 minutes. Place on hot coals. Put hot coals on Dutch oven lid. Check after 15 minutes. May use shorter time for baking.

INDEPENDENCE ROCK COBBLER

Crust:

2 1/2 c. Bisquick
Milk
2 T. sugar
2 tsp. cinnamon

Filling:

1 extra lg. can peaches, sliced
3 tsp. cinnamon
1/2 c. sugar

Spray inside Dutch oven with Pam or other cooking spray. Pour peaches and juice in bottom of Dutch oven. Sprinkle on cinnamon and sugar and stir slightly. In separate container, mix Bisquick with sugar and cinnamon and enough milk to make a soft dough. Drop by tablespoonfuls on top of peaches. Cook on a 1-inch base of coals, medium heat, and 3 inches of coals on top lid. Bake for 30-40 minutes. Check and rotate Dutch oven after first 15 minutes.

DUTCH OVEN COOKING

GOBBLED UP APPLE COBBLER

8 apples
Sugar
Cinnamon
Bisquick
Water/2 T. cornstarch
Milk

Adjust recipe to the size of Dutch oven. Wash and core apples. Slice into your greased Dutch oven. Apples should cover the bottom and be two to three inches deep. Cover apple slices with water/cornstarch mixture. Sprinkle with 1/4 cup or less of sugar and 1 teaspoon of cinnamon. In separate bowl, mix milk and Bisquick (may add sugar for sweeter biscuit). Dough should be thick enough to drop by spoonfuls on top of the apple mixture. Cook with hot coals from the fire. Put a few more coals on the top than on the bottom. Check often. Bake 45 minutes.

FRESH APPLE COBBLER

3 qts. apples, sliced
2 tsp. apple pie spice
1/2 c. water
1/4 c. margarine
1/2 c. brown sugar
1/2 c. sugar
1 yellow cake mix

Melt margarine in oven. Add apples, water and sugars. Bring to a boil. Add spice. Mix cake mix according to package and pour over apples. Bake 6-8 coals bottom, 14-20 coals top.

DUTCH OVEN COOKING

PEACH OR BLUEBERRY COBBLER

1 2/3-2 c. sugar
4 T. cornstarch
1 1/2 c. water
6 c. blueberries or sliced peaches
2 tsp. cinnamon
2 c. flour
1 T. baking powder
1 tsp. salt
2/3 c. milk
6 T. butter or oil

Mix water, sugar and cornstarch in seasoned oven. Stir and boil one minute. Add berries. **Topping:** Mix flour, baking powder and salt. Add milk and oil together. Stir until balls form. Drop by spoonfuls onto fruit. Sprinkle with cinnamon. Bake at 425 ° for 25-30 minutes until lightly browned (4-8 coals bottom, 15-25 top).

CHOCOLATE CHERRY CAKE

2 boxes chocolate cake mix
5 eggs
1 can sweetened condensed milk
2 cans evaporated milk
2/3 c. oil
1 can cherry pie filling

Grease and flour Dutch oven (use lots of flour). Mix all ingredients together except cherry pie filling. Pour into Dutch oven. Bake 1 1/2 hours or more on low to medium hot bed of coals, 3 inches on bottom and 3 inches on top lid. Check and rotate Dutch oven every 45 minutes and add more coals as necessary. The cake should come out when inverted. Top with cherry pie filling.

DUTCH OVEN COOKING

DAYBREAK ROLLS

18-20 Rhodes frozen dinner rolls
Grated peel of 1 orange or 2 lemons (dice & reserve leftover
    orange)
1 (6-oz.) can frozen orange juice concentrate, thawed (or
    lemonade)
$1/4$ c. sugar
$1/4$ c. butter

Line Dutch oven with foil. Melt butter in oven. Add orange peel,
diced orange, juice and sugar. Dip each roll into mixture, coating
heavily on all sides. Place lid on oven and put in a warm place to
rise 3 times in bulk, about 3-4 hours. Bake for about 35-45 minutes or until browned. Remove rolls by lifting foil from oven and
turning upside down on lid. **Hint:** To speed thawing, set oven in
the sun or put 1 briquet on bottom and 2 on top.

PULL APARTS

18-20 Rhodes frozen dinner rolls
$1/2$ c. butter
$2/3$ c. brown sugar
2 tsp. cinnamon
$2/3$ c. apple, chopped
$1/2$ c. nuts, chopped
$1/4$ c. golden raisins

Line Dutch oven with foil. Melt butter in oven. Add apples, brown
sugar, cinnamon, nuts and raisins. Dip each roll into mixture,
coating heavily on all sides. Place lid on oven and put in a warm
place to rise 3 times in bulk, about 3-4 hours. Bake for about 35-
45 minutes or until browned. Remove rolls by lifting foil from oven
and turning upside down on lid. **Hint:** To speed thawing, set oven
in the sun or put 1 briquet on bottom and 2 on top.

DUTCH OVEN COOKING

UPSIDE-DOWN WAGON CAKE

¹/₂ cube butter or margarine
1 (21-oz.) can sliced pineapple
¹/₃ c. brown sugar
Maraschino cherries
1 lemon-flavored cake mix
Eggs, oil & water for mix

Line 12-inch Dutch oven with foil. Put in butter or margarine and place on coals just long enough for butter to melt. Sprinkle brown sugar over melted butter. Place pineapple slices in a single layer over sugar mixture and place a maraschino cherry in center of each slice. Mix cake according to directions on package and pour over pineapple. Replace Dutch oven lid and cook until cake is done. Remove Dutch oven from coals and clean off ash with a whisk broom. With protective gloves, invert Dutch oven so lid rests on inverted lid holder. Remove Dutch oven. Carefully lift off foil and cut cake, serving directly from the lid, if desired.

Recipe Favorites

HERITAGE COOKING

Ethnic
recipes
passed
from the
Swedish,
Danish,
German,
Polish ...

INDEPENDENCE ROCK

Independence Rock was one of the most recognizable landmarks along the Oregon Trail. It was named by a group of fur traders who celebrated the 4th of July at this location in the late 1820's or early 1830's. Wagon trains arriving in the vicinity during early July either sped up or delayed their trip, so they could also celebrate Independence Day at this site. In place of fireworks, the pioneers filled the hubs of broken wagon wheels with gunpowder and placed them inside cracks in the rocks and ignited them.

Independence Rock became known as the "Great Register of the Desert", so named for the thousands of travelers who climbed the rock to carve their names in the red and white granite rock.

HERITAGE COOKING

The pioneers traveling the Oregon Trail were a cross-section of society including farmers, doctors, businessmen, politicians, missionaries, gamblers and anyone else with a desire to go West in search of a better life. With only their families and a few belongings, they combined their old ways with new ones and made their home in a new place. For many, this was an opportunity to own a house and land in a country that was very far away and very different from their homeland.

Preparing familiar foods was one way to ease homesickness. The recipes in this section were chosen to represent the different nationalities that settled in the West and Midwest in the years following the Civil War. Most of these ethnic dishes have been handed down for many generations. Many are traditional foods still enjoyed today during family dinners and holidays.❖

HERITAGE COOKING

GERMAN

SAUERBRATEN

4-lb. rump roast

Make brine of:

2 c. cider vinegar
3 c. water
1 c. brown sugar
1/2 lb. gingersnaps
Approx. 1 T. salt
2 T. mixed pickling spices
2 or 3 bay leaves
1 lg. onion, cut up

Heat vinegar and water; add all spices, gingersnaps and onion, salt and brown sugar. Bring to boiling point. Take a sharp knife and pierce meat (this enables brine to work through the meat). Put meat into hot brine and let stand for 4-5 days in refrigerator. Each day, turn meat morning and night. Do not use an aluminum pot. White enamel is best. The meat must be covered by the brine. Keep covered with lid. At the end of 4-5 days, take meat out of brine, drain and brown on all sides. Use a little fat in pot to brown. Heat brine, then add meat and boil until tender. Strain brine and thicken with cornstarch or flour for gravy.

GERMAN PRESSED CHICKEN
(For Sandwiches)

Boil chicken. Bone cooked chicken; then grind or put in blender, blending with a small amount of the broth, about 2 tablespoons to one cup of meat. Season with salt and pepper as desired. Pat firmly in square or oblong mold. Cover and let set overnight. Slice for sandwiches. This can be made in smaller quantities. Reserve extra broth for use in another dish.

140

BIEROCKS

1 1/2 lbs. hamburger
1 lg. head cabbage, finely chopped
1 lg. onion, chopped
Salt & pepper to taste
Your favorite bread dough

Make your favorite bread dough or you can use 1 package hot roll mix; let it rise. Lightly brown hamburger. Simmer cabbage and onion in small amount of water until well done. Drain both meat and vegetables. Mix together and cool. After dough has raised for 1 hour, roll out and cut into 4 or 5-inch squares about 1/4 inch thick. Place 1 tablespoonful or more of the meat and cabbage mixture in the center of dough square; pinch corners of dough together and seal seams. Place with seam side down on greased cookie sheet. Let rise 15-20 minutes. Bake at 350° to 375° for 25-30 minutes or until lightly browned.

WIENER SCHNITZEL

4 slices boneless calf cutlet
Flour
1 egg
Bread crumbs
Bacon fat or shortening
Salt
Pepper
Lemon
Parsley

Beat the cutlets to tenderize them. Then salt and pepper them. Beat the egg (water or milk may be added, if desired). The egg must remain liquid. Dip the cutlet first in the egg, then in the flour, then in the bread crumbs. Put enough shortening in a frying pan to keep the schnitzel from burning and let the pan get hot. The schnitzel must be cooked until brown on both sides and crisp dry. Serve the schnitzel with lemon slices and parsley.

HERITAGE COOKING

GERMAN GARLIC SAUSAGE

30 lbs. ground meat (2 parts pork, 1 part beef)
2 oz. black pepper
1/2 c. sugar
12 oz. salt
2 T. garlic salt

Mix dry ingredients and add to meat; mix well. Use sausage stuffer and pork casings to make sausages. Cut casing to desired length, about 18 inches.

KARTOFFEL PUFFER
(Potato Pancakes)

6 med. potatoes, grated
2 T. flour
1 1/2 tsp. salt
1/4 tsp. baking powder
1/8 tsp. pepper
2 eggs, beaten
1 T. grated onion
1 T. minced parsley

Combine 2 tablespoons flour with salt, baking powder and pepper. Combine eggs, onion and parsley and combine with the first mixture. Drain the potatoes that are grated and add to egg/flour mixture. Fry cakes in 1/4-inch hot fat until brown.

It is four a.m.; the sentinels on duty have discharged their rifles--the signal that the hours of sleep are over; every wagon and tent is pouring forth its tenants and smoke from fires begins to rise. Sixty men start from the corral and by five o'clock they have begun to move the herd of 5,000 cattle and horses toward the camp.
- Jesse Applegate, 1843

HERITAGE COOKING

KARTOFFEL AND KLOESSE

[German Potatoes and Dumplings]

Kloesse:

2 eggs, beaten
Salt to taste
1-1 1/2 c. flour
Water (same amount as eggs), measure in egg shell

Beat the eggs. Add the water and salt. Stir in the flour to get dough as stiff as can be stirred with a spoon (but still very soft). Dough is stiff enough if it doesn't cling to the mixing bowl. Boil cubed potatoes until half done in lightly salted water, approximately 1 teaspoon. Drop dumpling dough from a moistened spoon into boiling water and potatoes, dipping spoon in the hot water each time. Cook 5-10 minutes until done. Save drained water. Pour melted butter over potatoes and dumplings. For added flavor, saute chopped onion in the butter first. Serve with sour cream slightly diluted with the water drained from dumplings or serve with sauerkraut. To use with leftover potatoes, boil the dumplings separately 5-10 minutes and brown lightly in butter with the potatoes.

KREBBEL

[German Doughnuts]

Four cups flour, three eggs, one-half cup sugar, two cups milk, two teaspoons baking powder, two teaspoons salt. Mix same as other doughnuts; roll flat, cut in five-inch squares and make a slash in the center. Fry in hot lard and roll the cooked doughnuts in sugar to coat.

HERITAGE COOKING

ROGGENBROT

(German Rye Bread)

4 c. lukewarm water
2 pkgs. active dry yeast
3 tsp. salt
4 c. rye flour
4-5 c. white flour

Dissolve yeast in 1 cup lukewarm water. In a large kettle or bowl, mix 3 cups warm water and salt. Add yeast mixture. Let set 15 minutes. Add rye flour. Let mixture rise 1-1 ½ hours at room temperature. Stir in white flour until bread can be kneaded. Knead on floured surface until the dough begins to crack very slightly, about 20 minutes. For three 1-pound loaves: Divide dough into 3 equal portions. Place in three 1-pound greased loaf pans. Let rise in a warm place until doubled in bulk. Bake at 425° for approximately 15-20 minutes. Reduce heat to 350° to 375° and bake until done, approximately 40-45 minutes. Bread is done when it sounds hollow to thumping. (After bread has browned nicely, it is helpful to cover loaves with brown paper to prevent overbrowning.) Remove from pans. Brush top of loaves lightly with water; cover with foil or cloth to soften crust. **For a large, round European loaf:** After dough has been kneaded, place in greased kettle or bowl. Flip over to grease top surface. Let rise until double in bulk. Wet hands. Very carefully loosen dough from sides of kettle. Place on a greased cookie sheet which has flour generously scattered on it. Bake at 400° for 1 hour and 15 minutes. Heat may be reduced after browning. Loaf is done when it sounds hollow to thumping. Remove from oven. Scrape off excess flour. Brush top with water and cover to soften crust. Serve warm with butter.

ZWIEBACK

3 c. scalded milk
1 T. sugar
2 1/4 sticks oleo or butter
1/4 c. nondairy creamer
1 T. salt
2 eggs, beaten (opt.)
9 c. flour
2 tsp. sugar
2 pkgs. yeast
1/2 c. warm water

Dissolve 2 teaspoons sugar and 2 packages of yeast in 1/2 cup warm water. Then heat the first 3 ingredients until oleo is dissolved. Add the nondairy creamer and cool. Then add 6 cups flour with 1 tablespoon salt, beaten eggs and the yeast. Add remainder of the flour. Put dough on floured board and knead. Rest dough a few minutes; then knead some more. Place in a bowl. Let rise until doubled; then punch down. Let rise again. Then pinch off round balls. Put two together (on top) and put in pans. Bake at 350° or 375° for 20-25 minutes.

ROLLKOAKE CRULLERS

(Served with Watermelon)

2 eggs
1/2 c. shortening, melted
1/2 c. milk
2 tsp. salt
About 3 c. flour

Beat eggs; add melted shortening, milk and salt. Add enough flour to make a soft dough. Place dough on floured board and roll out very thin. Cut into 5 x 2-inch pieces. Cut a slit in the center of each piece and deep-fry in hot fat (375°) until done.

HERITAGE COOKING

APPLE KUCHEN

2 c. apples, peeled & chopped
1 c. granulated sugar
1 c. shortening
1 c. buttermilk
2 tsp. cinnamon
1/2 c. brown sugar
2 eggs, beaten
1 tsp. soda
1/2 tsp. baking powder
2 1/2 c. flour

Topping:

1/2 c. sugar
1/4 tsp. cinnamon
1/2 c. chopped nuts (opt.)

Mix together the dry ingredients. Add soda to the buttermilk and add to the dry ingredients along with the beaten eggs and cup of shortening. Mix well and add the apples. Pour batter into a 9 x 13-inch greased and floured pan. Sprinkle with topping and bake at 300° for 1 hour.

EIN GEMACHTEN ARBUS

(Sour Watermelon)

Use large wooden barrel. Cover bottom of barrel, using leaves of many fruit trees such as cherries, apple, plum, apricot and grape leaves from grape vines (whatever fruit trees you have may be used). Also bay leaves and dill. Cover the bottom of barrel with layer of leaves, then put in layer of watermelons. Use the small white winter melons, which are best for sour watermelons. Put in layers of each leaves and melons until barrel is filled. Cover with leaf mixture. Make a liquid of 1 gallon cold water and 1/2 cup pickling salt; mix well. Pour over melons and leaves until barrel is filled. Make sure all is covered. Then place a round piece of wood over the top and place large rock on top of wooden lid. Cover with heavy cloth. Let stand 5-6 weeks.

SCHNITZ SUPPE

[German Fruit Soup]

$1/2$ c. dried apricots
$1/2$ c. dried pears
$1/2$ c. white raisins
1 $1/2$ c. cold water
1 c. sweet cream
2 T. flour
$1/2$ c. dried prunes
$1/2$ c. dried peaches
1 cinnamon stick
Pinch of salt
2 T. sugar

Boil fruit, cinnamon stick and salt in water until fruit is tender, not overcooked. Make sure you keep enough water on fruit. Mix cream, sugar and flour. Add slowly to soup mixture until the soup thickens a little. Remove cinnamon stick. Eat hot or cold. Good with grebel.

SWEDISH

SWEDISH POTATIS KORV

(Potato Sausage)

1 sm. onion
2 lbs. ground pork*
1 lb. ground beef*
3 lbs. potatoes
2 T. salt
1 1/2 tsp. black pepper
1 1/2 tsp. allspice
1 tsp. ginger
1 c. water
5-6 yards hog casing

(*Three pound of ground beef may be substituted for pork and beef.) Grind finely, onions and raw peeled potatoes. Add all other ingredients except casing. Mix well! Stuff mixture into casings which have been cleaned and soaked in cold water. Do not fill casings too tightly because mixture expands when boiled. Cook in slowly boiled salted water 30-45 minutes. Cut sausage into pieces 3 inches long; serve immediately.

HERITAGE COOKING

KJOTTBOLLAR

(Swedish Meatballs)

Set out a cast iron (or heavy) skillet with fitted lid.

Lightly mix together in large bowl:

1 c. fine bread crumbs (divided)
1 lb. ground round steak, ground twice
1/2 c. ground pork, ground twice
1/2 c. veal, ground twice
1/3 c. finely grated carrots
1 egg, beaten
1/2 c. mashed potatoes
1 tsp. salt
1/2 tsp. brown sugar
1/4 tsp. pepper
1/4 tsp. allspice
1/4 tsp. nutmeg
1/8 tsp. cloves
1/8 tsp. ginger

Add all ingredients, mix by hand. Shape mixture into balls about 1 inch in diameter. Roll balls in remaining crumbs. Heat skillet; melt 2 tablespoons butter over low heat. Add the meatballs and brown on all sides. Shake pan frequently to brown evenly and to keep balls round. Cover and cook about 15 minutes or until meatballs are thoroughly cooked. Makes 3 dozen balls.

Find a great many companies continually in sight. In fact, it is one continued stream, as far as we can see both in front and rear the horizon is dotted with the white wagon covers of emigrants, like a string of beads.
- James Wilkins, 1849

PICKLED HERRING

1/2 c. white vinegar
1/3 c. white sugar
5 peppercorns
2 T. water
1-2 bay leaves
1 whole onion, cut thin slices
1 lg. salt herring

Clean and cut up herring in bite-sized pieces. Mix remaining ingredients and boil 1 minute; cool. Pour mixture over herring. Let marinate for 24 hours.

SWEDISH SALMON

1 whole salmon
Lg. sprig of dill

Cut small fins off. Cut salmon in half. Put in large pan of cold water and salt; add dill. Simmer approximately 20 minutes. Toothpick will come out easily.

Sauce:

1 c. whipped whipping cream
3 T. mayonnaise
2-3 T. fresh dill

Serve on platter with boiled potatoes and sauce on the side.

LUTFISK

Drop pieces of fish into salty water and keep at boiling point for about fifteen minutes, but do not boil hard. Cool and pick out all the bones and skin. Serve with a rich cream sauce made with one-fourth cup butter, one-fourth cup flour, two cups rich milk and salt and pepper to taste. Some like a little mustard in the sauce also.

LEFSE

Boil enough potatoes to make about four cups mashed and mash fine. Add half a cup of cream, a third a cup of butter and a teaspoon of salt; beat until light and let cool. Then add two cups of flour and one teaspoon sugar. Pinch off pieces of dough; roll out as for pie crust, as thin as possible, and bake on top of stove or pancake griddle until light brown, turning frequently to prevent scorching. Use moderate heat. When baked, place between clean cloths to keep from drying out. This is often eaten with lutfisk.

SWEDISH LIMPA RYE BREAD

2 1/4 c. warm water
3/8 c. molasses
1 1/2 tsp. salt
3 3/4 c. rye flour
3 3/4 c. white flour
2 pkgs. yeast
1/2 c. sugar
Rind of 1 orange
3 T. shortening

Dissolve yeast in warm water. Mix all ingredients together well. Knead for 10 minutes. Let rise once. Knead down and put in pans. Let rise again. Bake 30-35 minutes in 350° oven. Makes 4 loaves.

SWEDISH COFFEE BREAD

One and one-half quarts of milk, one cup bread starter, three cups sugar, one-half pound of butter, one teaspoonful ground cardamom seed, flour to make a soft dough, one teaspoon salt. Mix flour, warm milk, one cup of sugar and starter and set to rise. When light, add rest of sugar, cardamom seed, butter and flour and work it well. Let it rise again before forming into loaves or cakes. (See page 133 for bread starter recipe.)

HERITAGE COOKING

SWEDISH FLATBREAD

Combine two cups white flour or one cup each white and graham flour, one teaspoon salt and two tablespoons butter. Add boiling water to make a stiff dough, stirring continuously, and cool. Roll out thin on a board sprinkled with cornmeal and bake on top of stove, turning so as to brown evenly. Finish drying in oven for crisp flatbread.

ROTMOS

(Swedish Mashed Rutabaga & Potatoes)

2 lbs. pork sausage or ham (or 1 lb. of each)
3 tsp. salt
6 med. potatoes
1 med.-sized rutabaga
5 whole allspice

Boil meat with allspice in water to cover until nearly tender. Peel turnip and cut into small pieces. Cook for 30 minutes. Add potatoes, peeled and cut up; cook until done with meat. Remove meat and spice. Pour off most of the stock and mash the vegetables. Serve with sliced meat or cut some of the meat into small pieces and mix into mashed vegetables.

KOLDAIMA

Take one medium head of solid cabbage; boil until half done, take up and let drain until cold. Grind beef or veal fine and season with salt and pepper, a little butter, a little cream and a pinch of sugar. Work together until well mixed, then cut off the large leaves of the cabbage. Put a spoonful of the mixture on each leaf, shape into oblong rolls, folding the cabbage leaves over, and fasten with toothpicks. Brown in butter and boil slowly in just enough water to cover for about one and a half hours. May be served with brown gravy.

HERITAGE COOKING

SWEDISH HEAD CHEESE

Three pounds of pork shank, one pound veal shank, two pounds of beef shank, two pig's feet. Boil all together and when cool, slice in cubes; put in cloth and season with salt and pepper. Pour the hot liquid in which it cooked over it and let it stand in a pan with a heavy weight on it. When it is pressed, take it out of the cloth and put in a crock of brine.

FRUKT SOPPA
(Fruit Soup)

12 oz. prunes
1 c. raisins
4 T. pearl tapioca
1/2 c. sugar
3 sliced apples
2 sticks cinnamon
1 sliced lemon & orange
Canned pears
Canned pineapple
Frozen strawberries
Maraschino cherries

Soak prunes, raisins and tapioca overnight in 1 1/2 quarts water. In morning, add sugar, apples, lemon slices, orange slices and cinnamon. Cook slowly for an hour. Before serving, remove lemon and orange rinds; add canned and frozen fruits. Serve warm. (No Swedish Christmas is complete without fruit soup!)

DANISH

AEBLESKIVERS
(Danish Pancake Balls)

2 c. flour
$1/2$ tsp. salt
1 $1/2$ tsp. baking soda
1 tsp. baking powder
2 c. buttermilk
3 eggs, separated
1 tsp. vanilla
3 T. melted butter

Sift flour, salt, baking soda and baking powder into bowl. Add buttermilk, egg yolks and vanilla. Mix thoroughly. Beat egg whites until stiff, but not dry and fold into batter. Add buttermilk and butter and mix gently. Let stand about 30 minutes so that air bubbles can escape. Batter can be refrigerated for 2 days. Makes about 27 or 30 balls. **To cook:** It is necessary to use a heavy, cast iron Aebleskiver pan. The lighter aluminum ones tend to overheat and burn. Preheat the pan on medium heat (if using a gas burner, adjust the flame to about $1/2$-$3/4$ inch height). The Aebleskiver pan generally has about 7 semi-spherical cavities. Add about $1/2$-1 teaspoon of cooking oil, such as peanut oil, to each cavity. If it sizzles, the pan is ready. Add enough batter to each cavity to fill to barely even with the top. As the batter begins to cook a thin crust will begin to form at the sides of the cavities. Using a metal crochet hook, knitting needle, or small skewer, prick the forming crust and gently rotate the cooking ball slightly. Continue to rotate in small increments until a complete ball is formed and the entire surface is golden brown. Getting the heat of the pan adjusted properly is important. If too hot, the outside will cook too quickly, may burn and the center will be raw. When properly cooked, remove from pan and place on platter. Dust liberally with powdered sugar. Then place on individual plates (2 balls per plate). Aebleskivers may be covered with maple or fruit syrup or berry jam and eaten with sausage, bacon, ham, etc. for breakfast or brunch or as a dessert.

HERITAGE COOKING

KLEJNER CAKES

One pint sweet cream, one tablespoon sugar, two eggs, flour. Mix cream, eggs and sugar. Work in as much flour as it takes to slip dough off the hands. Roll dough out until the thickness of the back of a knife. Cut in strips five inches long and two inches wide. With a knife, make a slit in the middle and stick one end through the slit, so that the cake is twisted in the middle. Cook in hot grease until light brown (as for doughnuts).

DANISH SPICED MEAT ROLL

Clean a beef flank, cutting away all the bones and spread it out on a board. If too big, cut into desired sizes. Sprinkle with salt, pepper and a layer of sliced onions. Then roll up tight, sew with a strong thread and leave it in a strong salt brine for three days. Before cooking, tie well with string to keep it from falling apart. Place in a pan with water to cover and cook until tender. When done, put away into a heavy press for a day. Then remove string and slice in thin slices.

DANISH MEATBALLS

One pound ground beef, one pound ground pork sausage, one cup rich milk, five tablespoons flour, salt and pepper to taste, one large onion, minced. Mix meat, flour, salt, pepper and onion together, working in the milk a little at a time until the mixture slips off the spoon. Fry meatballs in hot lard over a slow fire, browning on all sides. When done, make a milk gravy and serve with potatoes or other vegetables.

HERITAGE COOKING

BALKEN BRIJ

1 lb. fat pork
2 lbs. pork liver
Water
1 T. salt
2 c. buckwheat flour
1 c. flour
Salt
Pepper

Cook pork and liver slowly until well done with salt, approximately 1 1/2 hours. Then grind meat finely in food chopper. Mix meat in pan with 6 pints water and heat. Mix flour and pepper. Stir until thickened to a consistency that will drop off spoon. Put in loaves and keep in refrigerator. Slice as needed and fry slices brown on both sides in a frying pan with very little shortening. Serve as a breakfast dish in place of bacon or sausage.

CZECH

CZECHOSLOVAKIAN CABBAGE SOUP

2 lbs. beef soup bones
1 c. chopped onion
3 carrots, pared & chopped
2 cloves garlic, chopped
1 bay leaf
2 lbs. beef short ribs
1 tsp. dried leaf thyme
$1/2$ tsp. paprika
8 c. water
1 head cabbage, coarsely chopped
2 (1-lb.) cans tomatoes
2 tsp. salt
$1/2$-$3/4$ tsp. Tabasco
$1/4$ c. chopped parsley
3 T. lemon juice
3 T. sugar
1 (1-oz.) can sauerkraut

Place bones, onion, carrots, garlic and bay leaf in roasting pan. Top with short ribs; sprinkle with thyme and paprika. Roast, uncovered, in 450° oven for 20-30 minutes or until brown. Transfer meat and vegetables into large kettle, using a small amount of water. Scrape browned meat bits from roaster into kettle. Add water, cabbage, tomatoes, salt and Tabasco. Bring to boil; cover and simmer 1-1 $1/2$ hours. Skim off fat. Add parsley, lemon juice, sugar and sauerkraut. Cook, uncovered, for 1 hour. Remove bones and ribs from kettle. Cool slightly; remove meat from bones. Cut meat into cubes; return to kettle and heat.

HERITAGE COOKING

JATERNICE
(Pork Sausage)

Cook the meat from the hog head, trimming away some of the fat. The heart and other lean parts of the hog may also be cooked, even the lungs. When meat is tender and comes off the bones of the head, remove from the broth and cool. Some cooks grind the meat but others like it finely chopped. To this chopped meat is added about 1 1/2 pounds raw ground liver. White bread soaked in water and squeezed of water. Old bread is best. Use about 1/3 bread to 2/3 meat. Add salt and pepper to taste, about 6 cloves garlic ground and rubbed to a paste. Do not overdo the garlic. Add 1 tablespoon marjoram. Mix all ingredients together thoroughly. Fill casings, tie each end of filled casing, then tie ends together making sausage rings. Put tied sausage rings into boiling broth and cook about 5 minutes or until raw liver is done. Do not crowd in kettle or boil too long or the casings will crack. When taken from broth, rinse in cold water and cool 1 layer deep. When cold, wrap in meat packages and store in deep freeze. These are good to eat cold or fried crisp brown in a skillet.

PRESSED BLOOD SAUSAGE

Boil head, snout, ears, tongue and a piece of meat from the neck. When done, cool and dice. Add rendered lard and cracklings, fresh blood (beaten to prevent clotting), salt, pepper, ginger and allspice fried in lard. Fill a cleansed pork stomach with this and boil an hour. When it can be pierced with a toothpick and no blood runs out, it is done. Place in a press in a warm place and put a weight on it. It is served with vinegar and pepper or vinegar and onion.

The evening is far less animated than the morning march; a drowsiness has fallen apparently on man and beast; teamsters fall asleep on their perches and even when walking by their teams. . .
- Jesse Applegate, 1843

JELITA

(Blood Sausage)

1 lb. barley (not pearl)
1 c. ground pork fat
1 1/2 c. minced onion
1 qt. raw blood
1 clove garlic
1 tsp. caraway seed
1/2 tsp. marjoram
Salt & pepper to taste

Reserve 2 quarts of prepared pork sausage. To this add all of the above ingredients, adding the blood last. Mix thoroughly and stuff into casings, loose. Tie ends and cook until blood will not show raw color on toothpick when pricked into casing. **To prepare pork sausage:** Cook barley in 2 quarts water in baking pan or small roaster pan in 400° oven until tender. Add water if it cooks out before barley is done. Cook onion in ground pork fat until the fat is melted down and onion is tender. Use all the fat the onion was cooked in, because the barley will absorb it, otherwise it would be dry and tasteless.

CZECH RYE BREAD

2 pkgs. (2 T.) dry yeast
6 c. warm water
2 T. caraway seeds
3 c. rye flour
1 c. white flour
2 T. salt
1/4 c. melted shortening
3/4 c. dry milk
1 c. rye flour
12 c. sifted white flour (10 c. unsifted)

Dissolve yeast in warm water. Add caraway seed, 3 cups rye flour and 1 cup white flour; beat until smooth and let rise until bubbly and doubled in bulk. Then add salt, melted shortening, dry milk, rye flour, 12 cups white flour (or enough to make a stiff dough, usually 12 cups sifted or about 10 cups unsifted). Knead, place in a greased bowl and let rise. Once is good, but twice is better. Shape into six loaves. Let rise about 15 minutes. Bake at 400° for 45 minutes to one hour.

HERITAGE COOKING

KOLACHES

Scald one pint of milk; let cool to lukewarm. Dissolve one and one-half cakes compressed yeast in one-fourth cup lukewarm water to which one teaspoon of sugar has been added. Let rise while milk cools. Add dissolved yeast to cooled milk and make a sponge. Let rise until light. Cream together one cup sugar and one cup butter. Add three egg yolks and two whole eggs, well beaten, and two teaspoons salt. Add to the sponge and mix well. Stir in flour enough to handle well. Let rise until light and roll out to one-half inch thickness. Cut with a biscuit cutter. Make a depression in the center and fill. Let rise and bake in a quick oven. Any of the following fillings can be used: **Fruit Filling:** Mash stewed prunes. Add sugar and cinnamon to taste and sprinkle with coconut or chopped nuts. Apricots, peaches, apples or any canned fruit may also be used. **Poppy Seed Filling:** Grind poppy seed and boil it in just enough water to keep moist. Then add sugar, cinnamon and maple syrup to taste; raisins and three or four gingersnaps, ground. **Cottage Cheese Filling:** Combine grated rind of lemon, one-half cup sugar, one tablespoon cream, two egg yolks and one pint of dry cottage cheese.

BABOVKA
(Poppy Seed Roll)

1 1/2 c. warm milk
1/4 c. sugar
3 egg yolks
4 c. or enough flour to make stiff dough
1 cake yeast
1/4 c. melted butter
Dash of mace or grated lemon rind for flavor

Beat and work dough thoroughly. Let rise until double in bulk. Turn out on floured board and roll out to a 16-inch square. Brush with beaten egg, then spread 1 can "Solo" prepared poppy seed filling or use your own prepared poppy seed filling, if desired. Roll up like jellyroll. Place in greased ring mold and let rise until double. Bake in 350° oven 1 hour.

HERITAGE COOKING

HOUSKA
[Christmas Twist]

2 1/2 c. milk
1 c. shortening
1 c. sugar
1 tsp. salt
2 cakes compressed yeast or 2 pkgs. dry yeast
1/4 c. lukewarm water
1 T. sugar
Flour
2 eggs, beaten
1 c. raisins
1/2 c. currants
1/2 c. almonds or walnuts, chopped

Scald milk. Add shortening, sugar and salt. Cool to lukewarm. Dissolve yeast in water. Add tablespoon of sugar and enough flour to make a soft batter. Add to scalded milk. Add beaten eggs. Add about 5 cups of flour, fruit and nuts. Dough should be medium stiff as for kolaches. Let rise. Divide dough in half for 2 Houskas, each half in three graduated portions as 6-5-3. First portion (6) divide into 3 strands. Braid them. Place on one side of a greased 10 x 14-inch pan. Take second portion (5) and divide into 3 strands, braiding. Put this braid on top of first braid. Take last portion (3) and divide into 2 strands. Twist these like a rope and put on top of last braid. Repeat with second half of dough for second Houska, putting it next to the first Houska on the same pan. Beat 1 egg and brush tops of Houskas. Sprinkle with poppy seed. Let rise before baking at 350° for 1 hour.

. . .from the midst of dark pine forests, the isolated snowy peaks (of the Cascade Mountains) were looking out like giants. They served us for grand beacons to show the route at which we advanced in our journey.
- John C. Fremont, 1843

HERITAGE COOKING

POLISH

KIELBASA

(Polish Sausage)

1 1/2 lbs. pork loin or butt
1/2 lb. veal
Salt & pepper
1 bud of garlic
1 tsp. whole mustard seed
3 T. water

Remove meat from bones. Cut into small pieces; run through coarse knife of food grinder. Add 3 tablespoons of water. Pound the garlic; add the seasoning. Mix very thoroughly and stuff casing. The sausage is then ready for smoking. If you do not have facilities for smoking, place the sausage in baking dish. Cover with cold water and bake in 350° oven until the water is absorbed.

KAPU'SNIAK ZE 'SWIEZEJ KAPUSTY

(Fresh Cabbage Soup)

5 slices bacon, diced
1 lb. cabbage, chopped
2 carrots, sliced
2 potatoes, sliced
1 stalk celery, sliced
1 1/2 qts. water
2 T. flour
2 T. butter or margarine, room temperature
Salt & pepper

Fry bacon until golden, but not crisp, in a 3-quart saucepan. Add vegetables and water. Simmer 30 minutes or until vegetables are tender. Blend flour into butter; stir into soup. Bring soup to boiling, stirring. Season to taste with salt and pepper. If desired, serve with dumplings or pierogi. Makes 6-8 servings.

HERITAGE COOKING

KLUSKI Z KAPUSTA PO POLSKI

(Polish Noodles & Cabbage)

1/4 c. butter or margarine
1/2 c. chopped onion
4 c. chopped or sliced cabbage
1 tsp. caraway seed
1/2 tsp. salt
1/8 tsp. pepper
8 oz. egg noodles
1/2 c. dairy sour cream (opt.)

Melt butter in large skillet. Add onion; saute until soft. Add cabbage; saute 5 minutes or until crisp-tender. Stir in caraway seed, salt and pepper. Meanwhile, cook noodles; drain well. Stir noodles into cabbage. Add sour cream, if desired. Cook 5 minutes longer, stirring frequently.

CZARNINA

(Duck Soup)

1 (5 to 6-lb.) duck, cut up
1 qt. duck blood
1 1/2 lbs. pork loin back ribs
2 qts. water
2 tsp. salt
1 stalk celery
1 sprig parsley
5 whole allspice
2 whole cloves
1 lb. dried prunes, pitted
1/2 c. raisins
1 sm. tart apple, chopped
2 T. flour
1 T. sugar
1 c. whipping cream or dairy sour cream
Salt & pepper
Lemon juice or vinegar

Purchase duck and blood from butcher. The blood will contain vinegar. (If preparing your own poultry, put 1/2 cup vinegar into glass bowl with blood to prevent coagulation; set aside). Cover duck and back ribs with water in a large kettle. Add salt. Bring to boiling. Skim off foam. Put celery, parsley, allspice and cloves into cheesecloth bag and add to soup. Cover and cook over low heat until meat is tender, 1 1/2 hours. Remove spice bag from kettle. Discard bones. Cut up meat. Return meat to soup. Add prunes, raisins and apple; mix. Cook 30 minutes. With beater, blend flour and sugar into cream until smooth. Add blood mixture, a little at a time, continuing to beat. Add about 1/2 cup hot soup stock to blood and cream mixture, blending thoroughly. Pour mixture slowly into the soup, stirring constantly, until soup comes to just boiling. Season to taste with salt, lemon, pepper or vinegar. Serve with homemade noodles, if desired.

HERITAGE COOKING

EGG NOODLES

Put one cup of flour on a dusted board and form into a hill with a hole in the center. Drop in one egg and one-fourth teaspoon salt. Mix and add one-half eggshell of water. Knead until dough is smooth, then roll thin and put on a floured cloth to dry for several hours. Sprinkle dough lightly with flour and roll tight. Cut the rolled dough into thin noodles, toss to separate and dry. Boil in salted water until noodles rise to the top; drain and rinse in cold water. Store what is not used immediately uncooked in a jar.

CHEESE CAKES

Force two cups dry cottage cheese through cheesecloth. Add two eggs, two tablespoons cream and one-fourth cup sugar and beat thoroughly; then add one-fourth cup raisins and one cup flour. Roll into balls, make an indentation in the center and fry in butter. Fill the center with fruit or sour cream and sprinkle with cinnamon.

PIEROGI

Three cups flour, three beaten eggs, one teaspoonful salt, one-half cup milk, cottage cheese sweetened with a little sugar and seasoned with salt. Mix flour, eggs, salt, milk and a little water, if needed, to make the consistency of noodle dough. Knead well, roll out and cut into three or four-inch circles. Fill one side of each with about two tablespoonfuls cottage cheese. Fold over other side, seal or crimp like pie crust and drop one or two at a time into boiling water. Keep turning them so that they don't stick to the bottom of the pan. Boil five or six minutes or until they rise, then fry lightly on each side in butter and onions.

HERITAGE COOKING

PRUNE SOUP

Two cups of dried prunes, a handful of raisins; cook in water to cover well. Season with a pinch of salt and add a tablespoonful of sugar or to taste. When done, add dumplings. Serve with a half cupful of sweet cream over it.

SZARLOTKA

(Polish Apple Cake)

3/4 c. butter or margarine
4 1/2 c. flour
4 egg yolks
8 T. sugar
1/2 tsp. salt
4-5 T. sour cream
3 1/2 tsp. baking powder
8 peeled, sliced & cored apples
1/2 c. sugar
Several T. water
1/2 tsp. grated lemon rind
Pinch of cinnamon
Pinch of nutmeg
Powdered sugar

Cut butter into flour, a little at a time, until mixture looks like cornmeal. Add egg yolks, sugar, salt, sour cream and baking powder. When combined, chill dough. In a saucepan, cook apples with sugar and water until mixture thickens. Add cinnamon, nutmeg and lemon rind. Divide dough into 2 parts. Roll out to fit **well greased** 9 x 13-inch pan. Place bottom dough in pan. Top with apple mixture. Cover with remaining dough. Seal edges. Brush top with egg whites. Bake at 375° for 45 minutes or until top is golden. When cooled, cut into squares. Dust with powdered sugar.

IRISH

IRISH STEW

2 lbs. lamb
1/2 lb. bacon
9 med. potatoes, peeled
10-12 sm. onions, sliced
Salt & pepper
2 c. cold water

Cut meat into 3/4-inch cubes. Trim fat as much as possible. Cut bacon into 1-inch pieces. Place a layer of bacon, potatoes, onions and lamb. Sprinkle with seasonings. Repeat layers, finishing with potatoes. Add water and let it come to a boil. Remove any scum. Cover and simmer gently for 2 1/2 hours. The potatoes should be cooked to a pulp.

PASTIES

Rich pastry, enough for double crust pie
3/4 lb. beef (good quality)
2 med. potatoes, sliced
1 med. onion, sliced
2 turnips, if desired
Salt & pepper to taste
Generous amount of parsley
Water

Roll out pastry in square shape or long oval. Cover half of it with a layer of sliced potatoes and a layer of onions. Add layer of turnips. Add salt, pepper and parsley; sprinkle with water. Lay strips of meat (size of finger) over top and around sides of vegetables. Fold other half of pastry over meat and vegetables forming a triangle and crimp well. May also be made in individual sized servings. Slit a few vents in the top of pastry and bake in hot 450° oven for 10 minutes. Reduce heat to 350° and continue baking for about 50 minutes or until vegetables pierced with fork are tender. Finely shaved suet may be placed over meat, if desired. Ground beef may be substituted but is not so tasty.

IRISH SODA BREAD

3 c. flour, sifted
2/3 c. sugar
1 tsp. salt
1 T. baking powder
1 tsp. baking soda
1 1/2 c. seedless raisins
2 eggs, beaten
2 c. buttermilk
2 T. shortening or margarine, melted

Preheat oven to 350°. Sift flour, baking powder, baking soda and salt into a bowl; stir in raisins. Combine eggs, buttermilk and melted shortening or margarine and add to dry ingredients, mixing with a fork until flour mixture is moistened. Turn batter into a greased loaf pan and bake for about 1 hour or until a toothpick inserted comes out clean. Remove from pan and cool on rack.

HERITAGE COOKING

PIONEER SODA BREAD

To make dough, mix 1 teaspoon of baking soda with 1 cup of warm water; add 2 ¹/₄ cups of flour and 1 teaspoon of salt. Knead well. The dough may be used at once or allowed to rise overnight in a warm place. In either case, flatten dough to a thickness of 1 inch. Place on greased cookie sheet and bake in a hot oven for about 25 minutes.

IRELAND PRATIE OATEN
(Potato Cakes)

2 c. potatoes, freshly mashed
2 T. + butter, melted
Salt
2 eggs, beaten
3 T. light cream
Bread crumbs

Form cold, mashed potatoes into patties; dip in batter, roll in bread crumbs and brown in melted butter. Serve warm with lemon. Called **Fadge** in the north.

The environs of our new home (Oregon City), sur-rounded by giant fir trees, the healthful sea breezes, the strange sights and sounds were sources of continual thought. The long dis-tance that separated us from our old home in the Mississippi Valley, precluded any form of home sickness and our united efforts were whol-ly set upon the building of a home.
- Sarah Cummings, 1845

COLCANNON

6 med. potatoes, peeled & quartered
4 c. shredded cabbage
1 c. green onions, chopped
$1/4$ c. butter
$1/8$ tsp. pepper
$1/2$-$3/4$ c. milk
1 tsp. salt
1 T. snipped parsley

Cook potatoes in large amount of salted, boiling water until tender, about 20 minutes. Drain. Meanwhile, cook cabbage in small amount of boiling water for 15 minutes; drain. Simmer chopped green onions in the milk for about 10 minutes. Mash potatoes using electric mixer. Beat in butter and as much milk as necessary to make fluffy. Add salt and pepper. Stir in cabbage. Top with parsley. Serve with butter or gravy. Makes 6 servings.

HERITAGE COOKING

Recipe Favorites

HOME REMEDIES

Picture courtesy of Scotts Bluff National Monument.

Concoctions for common ailments and daily beauty regimens.

Barlow Cutoff

Mount Hood, the highest peak in Oregon, was frequently noted in pioneer diaries as "the grandest sight we had yet seen." Travelers on the early Oregon Trail went north of Mount Hood and rafted down the Columbia River. In 1845, Samuel Barlow, an early pioneer from Kentucky, requested toll rights for a land route he had marked to the south of the mountain. Though safer than rafting the river, the Barlow Road plunged so steeply in places that the settlers had to lower their wagons with ropes wrapped around trees.

The lush, richly timbered Willamette Valley on the other side of Mount Hood marked the end of the Oregon Trail for most of its travelers. The rich soil and gentle climate produced abundant crops and was often called the "pioneer's paradise."

HOME REMEDIES

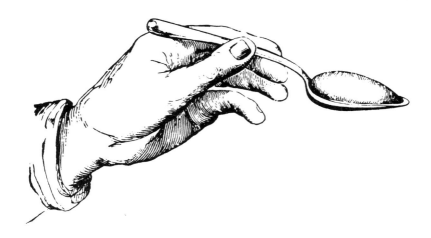

After all the food, clothing, tools and other provisions were packed into the wagons, little room was left for anything else such as medicinal supplies. While on the trail, the pioneers were faced with situations they never could have imagined: sunburn, snake bites, mosquito bites, snow blindness and frostbite. In some cases, they could draw on remedies learned at home; however, more often they were guided only by their intuition.

Sometimes the remedies appeared to be more dangerous than the afflictions. Gunpowder was applied to warts; turpentine was poured on open cuts; a teaspoon of sugar moistened with turpentine was supposed to relieve rheumatism; goose grease, skunk oil and lard were basic liniments. The following section of remedies and beauty tips illustrates that both folklore and ingenuity were needed to survive the early days on the frontier.❖

HOME REMEDIES

CONCOCTIONS FOR AILMENTS

COUGH SYRUP

1. One ounce horehound leaves, one ounce wild cherry bark, one ounce hops. Mix all three together; add two quarts of cold water. Simmer slowly or until it is reduced down to about one quart. Strain, then add one cup honey, one cup sugar; boil again until you have one pint thick-like syrup. Children like it and very good for coughs.

2. Mix one teaspoon of white whiskey with a pinch of sugar; heat over fire and drink.

3. Eat a mixture of honey and vinegar.

4. Take some rock candy with tea.

TO CURE HOARSENESS

Beat well the whites of two eggs and two tablespoonfuls of white sugar. Grate in half a nutmeg; add a pint of lukewarm water. Stir well and drink often. Repeat the preparation if necessary.

SORE THROAT

1. Bake onions in an open fireplace; then tie them around your throat.

2. Gargle with honey and vinegar.

3. Gargle with salty water.

4. Put a drop of kerosene on a lump of sugar and eat it.

5. Gargle with a half cup water, two tablespoons vinegar and a half teaspoon of salt.

HOME REMEDIES

ARTHRITIS

1. Drink a mixture of honey, vinegar and whiskey.

2. Make a tea from either the seeds or leaves of alfalfa.

3. A magnet draws it out of the body.

ASTHMA

1. Suck salty water up your nose.

2. Smoke or sniff rabbit tobacco.

3. Swallow a handful of spider webs rolled into a ball.

4. Smoke strong tobacco until you choke.

5. Drink a mixture of honey, lemon juice and whiskey, using about 1 tablespoon of each.

6. Gather leaves from ginseng; dry and powder them. Put the powder in a pan, place a hot coal on top of it and inhale the smoke.

BLEEDING

1. Place a spider web across the wound.

2. Apply a poultice of spirit turpentine and brown sugar to the wound.

3. Apply lamp black directly to the wound.

4. Use a mixture of soot from the chimney and lard.

5. Use kerosene oil, but be careful not to add too much or it will blister the skin.

HOME REMEDIES

BROKEN ARM

Make a mixture of red clay and water. Put splints on each side of the arm and plaster it up with the clay. When the clay dries, put the arm in a sling.

BURNS

1. Put hot coals on the burned place and pour water over them. The steam will draw the fire out.

2. Powder hot coals and put this warm powder on the burn.

3. Boil chestnut leaves and place the resulting ooze on the burn.

4. Take table salt and dissolve it in warm water. Wrap the burn in gauze and keep it constantly warm and moist with applications of the salt water.

5. The scrapings of a raw white potato will draw the fire.

6. Put axle grease on the burned area.

HOME REMEDIES

CHEST CONGESTION

1. Make a poultice of kerosene, turpentine and pure lard (the latter prevents blistering). Use wool cloth soaked with the mixture. Place cheesecloth on chest for protection and then add the wool poultice.

2. Make an onion poultice by roasting an onion, then wrapping it in spun wool rags and beating it so that the onion juice soaks the rags well. Apply these rags to chest.

3. Render the fat of a polecat. Eat two or three spoonfuls. This brings up the phlegm.

4. Mix up hog lard, turpentine and kerosene. Rub it on chest.

5. Wear a flannel shirt with turpentine and lard on it all winter.

CRAMPS

To cure cramps in the feet, turn your shoes upside down before going to bed.

CROUP

Squeeze the juice out of a roasted onion and drink.

HOME REMEDIES

EARACHE

1. Dissolve table salt in lukewarm water and pour this into ear. This dissolves the wax which is causing the pain.

2. Put either wet ashes wrapped in a cloth or hot ashes in a sack on ear and hold there.

3. Roast cabbage stalks and squeeze the juice into ear.

4. Warm a spoonful of urine and put a few drops in ear.

5. Hold your head close to a hot lamp.

6. Put a few ashes in an old rag. Dampen it with hot water and sleep with your head on it.

EYE AILMENTS

Put a few drops of castor oil in eye.

FEVER

Boil two roots of wild ginger in a cup of water; strain and drink.

BEE STINGS

Put moist snuff, mud, tobacco juice, or red clay on it.

CHIGGER BITES

To relieve itching and infection, rub chewed snuff or tobacco over the bites.

HOME REMEDIES

SPIDER BITES

If bitten by a black widow spider, drink liquor heavily from 3 p.m. to 7 p.m. You won't get drunk, you'll be healed.

BUGS

For head lice (cooties), shingle hair close and use kerosene. For chinches or bed bugs, burn sulfur in a closed house.

FRETFUL CHILD

Boil catnip leaves to make a tea and give the child about a quarter cup. Use one cup of leaves to a pint of water to make him sleep.

HEADACHES

1. Tie a flour sack around your head.

2. Put turpentine and beef tallow in a bandage and tie it tightly around your head.

3. Smear brow with crushed onions.

4. When you get your hair cut, gather up all the clippings. Bury them. Old-timers would never allow their hair to be burned or thrown away as it was too valuable.

HEART TROUBLE

Eat ramps and garlic. You can eat them cooked or raw.

HOME REMEDIES

INFLAMMATION

Bind salty fat meat to a stone bruise or a thorn in the foot to draw out the inflammation. A poultice of clay will do the same thing.

To kill infection, pour some turpentine or kerosene mixed with sugar on the affected area.

FRECKLES

1. Buttermilk and lemon juice mixed together and put on freckles will remove them.

2. Put sap from a grapevine on them.

3. Make a poultice of eggs, cream and epsom salts and spread on the freckles. Take off after it dries.

MEASLES

1. Any herb tea will break them out.

2. Keep the person home and out of the cold. Then give him some whiskey to drink. Use a few drops for tiny children and a tablespoon for adults. It will make the person sweat.

NAIL PUNCTURE

1. Pour kerosene oil over the cut or soak it in same three times a day. This will also remove the soreness.

2. Mix lard with soot from the chimney, thin with turpentine and pack around the wound.

HOME REMEDIES

NOSEBLEED

1. Take a small piece of lead and bore a hole in it. Put a string through the hole, tie it and wear it around your neck. Your nose won't bleed again.

2. Place a coin directly under the nose between the upper lip and the gum and press tightly.

3. Hang a pair of pot hooks about your neck.

PNEUMONIA

1. To bring down the fever, put some quinine and hog lard on a cloth and put it on your chest.

2. Give the person two teaspoonfuls of oil rendered from a skunk.

3. Make an onion poultice to make the fever break. Then give the person whiskey and hot water.

RHEUMATISM

1. Drink a tea made from the seeds or leaves of the alfalfa plant.

2. Cook garlic in your food to ease the pain.

3. Carry a buckeye or an Irish potato until it gets hard.

STOMACH TROUBLE

1. Make a tea of wild peppermint and drink it.

2. Drink some blackberry juice or wine.

3. Drink some juice from kraut left over after cooking.

HOME REMEDIES

SORES

1. Put butter around the sore so a dog will lick it. The dog's saliva will cure it.

2. Put a little lard or something equally greasy on the sore. Then dust the sore with sulfur. The grease will hold the sulfur on.

TREATMENT FOR DIPHTHERIA

One teaspoonful sulphur in a wine glass of water. Gargle the throat and swallow a small quantity.

YELLOW JAUNDICE

Scrape a cow's horn, boil the scrapings and drink.

PREVENTIVES, CURE-ALLS

Spring Tonics:

1. Mix together some sulfur and molasses and eat it.

2. Eat rhubarb once a week.

Salves:

Take about two tablespoons of mutton tallow and heat it up in a frying pan with about six balm of Gilead buds. Mash the buds up while the mixture cools and when the grease is all out of the buds, strain the mixture. Put it in a jar and cover it. The salve is clear and will keep for years.

HOME REMEDIES

BED-WETTING

For bed-wetting, feed the child a couple of elderberries or red sumac ("shumate") berries before bedtime.

NIGHTMARES

Place a Bible under your pillow and you will never have nightmares.

TONSIL TROUBLE

1. Gargle with salt water.

2. To burn out tonsils, paint them several times a day for several months with iodine and turpentine.

TOOTHACHE

1. Put drops of vanilla straight from the bottle on the tooth.

2. Put some homemade tobacco in a corncob pipe. Light it and draw the smoke over the tooth.

3. Hold whiskey or turpentine on the tooth.

WORMS

Take the shells of a hen's egg and bake them until they turn brown and brittle. Crumble them up fine and mix the particles with syrup and butter. Feed this to the sick person every morning for one week. The particles cut the worms to pieces. This remedy also works for dogs and other animals.

HOME REMEDIES

CREAM SOUP FOR INVALIDS

One pint boiling water, one-half teacup cream; add broken pieces of toasted bread and a little salt.

EGG GRUEL FOR INVALIDS

Beat the yolk of an egg with one tablespoon sugar, beating the white separately. Add one teacup boiling water to the yolk, then stir in the white and add any kind of seasoning. Especially good for a cold.

RICE JELLY FOR INVALIDS

Boil a fourth of a pound of rice flour with a half pound of loaf sugar in one quart of water until it becomes one mass; strain off the jell and let it cool.

BEEF TEA FOR INVALIDS

Mince one pound of good lean beef and put into a jar with one teacupful cold water; cork closely and set in a boiler or steamer to cook. It will require three or four hours; strain and season.

GRUEL FOR INVALIDS

Have a pint of water boiling in a skillet; stir up 3 or 4 large spoonfuls of nicely sifted oatmeal, rye or Indian corn in cold water. Stir it into the skillet while the water boils. Let it boil 8 or 10 minutes. Throw in a large handful of raisins to boil if the patient is well enough to bear them. When put in a bowl, add a little salt, white sugar and nutmeg.

HOME REMEDIES

BEAUTY REGIMENS

SOAP

Five pounds lard or five and one-half pounds cracklings, one can lye, one and one-half gallons water. Stir occasionally the first day, then set for three days. Cook until clear. Let set until hard and cut into bars.

LYE SOAP

2 pecks water
2 cans lye
5 lbs. grease (lard)

Combine ingredients. Cook until thick. Take a feather and dip in the soap. If the lye eats the feather, it needs more grease.

HAIR INVIGORATOR

Bay rum, one pint; alcohol, one-half pint; castor oil, one-half ounce; carbonate of ammonia, one-quarter ounce; tincture of cantharides, one-half ounce; mix them well. This mixture will promote the growth of the hair and prevent it from falling out.

TO HELP HAIR GROW

Break a section of a grape vine, set in a bottle and let the juice drain. Rub the juice in your hair.

HOME REMEDIES

SHAMPOO FOR HAIR

(This recipe is over 100 years old.)

Shave up to 3 tablespoons white soap, 3 teaspoons powdered borax, 3 teaspoons ammonia and 2 pints boiling water. Let it stand on the stove until all is dissolved. Use 1/2-1 cupful to a wash.

OIL TO MAKE THE HAIR CURL

1 pound olive oil, 1 drachm oil of organum, 1 1/2 drachm oil rosemary.

FOR WRINKLES IN THE SKIN

1 ounce white wax, 2 ounces honey, 2 ounces juice of 2 lily bulbs. The foregoing melted and stirred together will remove wrinkles.

FACE POWDER

Take of wheat starch, 1 pound; powdered orris root, 3 ounces; oil of lemon, 30 drops; oil of bergamot, oil of cloves, each 15 drops. Rub thoroughly together.

GOOD HAND LOTION

1 cup glycerin, 1 cup bay rum, 2 cups rose water, 1/2 ounce tincture of benzoin, 1 large tablespoon quince seed. Mix all in order given.

HOME REMEDIES

CHAPPED HANDS

Powdered starch is an excellent preventive of chapping of the hands when it is rubbed over them after washing. It will also prevent the needle in sewing from sticking and becoming rusty. It is advisable to have a small box of it in the workbox or basket and near your washbasin.

CHAPPED HANDS

Equal parts of lemon juice, camphor and glycerine makes a splendid wash for chapped hands.

HAND LOTION

An excellent preparation for the hands; 5 cents worth quince seed, simmer in one pint of water; strain and add equal quantity of pure glycerine and small portion of rose water. Shake well.

WASH FOR A BLOTCHED FACE

Rose water, three ounces; sulphate of zinc, one drachm; mix. Wet the face with it, gently dry it and then touch it over with cold cream, which also gently dry off.

TO CLEAR A TANNED SKIN

Wash with a solution of carbonate of soda and a little lemon juice; then with the juice of unripe grapes.

HOME REMEDIES

PEARL WATER FOR THE FACE

Put half a pound best Windsor soap scraped fine into half a gallon of boiling water; stir it well until it cools; add a pint of spirits of wine and half an ounce of oil of rosemary; stir well. This is a good cosmetique, and will remove freckles.

PEARL DENTIFRICE

Prepared chalk, one-half pound; powdered myrrh, two ounces; camphor, two drachms; orris root powdered, two ounces. Moisten the camphor with alcohol and mix all well together.

BANDOLINE

To one quart of rose-water, add an ounce and a half of gum tragacanth; let it stand forty-eight hours, frequently straining it, then strain through a coarse linen cloth; let it stand two days and again strain; add to it a drachm of oil of roses; used by ladies dressing their hair to make it lie in any position.

CURE FOR CORNS

Take a well ripened lemon, roll and squeeze until the juices are well liquified, then open an end of the lemon and squeeze the juice into a glass vial. Add to the juice three or six pearl buttons, according to size, such as are used on linen or cambric underwear. In a few days it will be found the lemon juice has eaten up or dissolved the buttons so they can be mashed between the thumb and finger. Shake the mixture well, then apply it to the corn. A few applications will conquer the most stubborn settler and give permanent relief. This is a remedy easily prepared and contains no poisonous substance, so all who desire can use it without fear of evil consequences.

HOME REMEDIES

TO REMOVE WARTS

The best application is said to be that of mono-hydrated nitric acid. The ordinary acid should not be used, because its caustic effects extend much farther than the points touched, while the action of the stronger acid here recommended is limited to the parts to which it is actually applied. Nitrate of silver is also frequently used with advantage and of late a concentrated solution of chloral has been spoken of as efficient in destroying warts.

WASHING FLUID

One can Babbit's lye dissolved in one gallon rain water; let cool and add 10 cents worth of salts of tartar and 10 cents worth of ammonia. Use in washing and boiling water, a half teacupful to one-half boiler of water.

HOUSEHOLD TIPS

SHOE POLISH

To restore the color of black kid boots, take a small quantity of black ink, mix it with the white of an egg and apply with a soft sponge.

TO CLEAN SILVER

Table silver should be cleaned at least once or twice a week and can easily be kept in good order and polished brightly in this way: Have your dish pan half full of boiling water; place your silver in so that it may become warm; then with a soft cloth dipped into the hot water, soaped and sprinkled with powdered borax, scour the silver well; then rinse in clean hot water; dry with a clean, dry cloth.

HOME REMEDIES

TO WHITEN KNIFE HANDLES

The ivory handles of knives sometimes become yellow from being allowed to remain in dish water. Rub them with sandpaper until white. If the blades have become rusty from careless usage, rub them also with sandpaper and they will look as nice as new.

REMOVE COFFEE STAINS

Apply glycerine to coffee stains, wash the spots in lukewarm water and iron until dry.

SOLUTION FOR TAKING OUT STAINS

Half pound chloride of lime, one and a half pounds salt soda; put both in a jar and pour one gallon of boiling water over. Stir until dissolved, then strain and bottle. Wet the stain with the solution and lay in sun.

HINTS ON WASHING

Clothes should not be soaked overnight; it gives them a grey look and the soiled parts lying against the clean portions streak them. Rub the clothes in warm, not hot, water, for hot water sets, in place of removing the dirt. Wash flannels in lukewarm water and avoid rubbing soap upon flannels.

Today we set foot in Oregon Territory. . . "The land of promise."
- Theodore Talbot, 1843

190

HOME REMEDIES

RUST STAINS

Light iron rust, ink or mildew may be removed by washing the spots with lemon juice and salt and exposing to bright sunshine. If one application does not prove effective, repeat the operation until stains disappear. If they are very deep, use citric acid instead of the lemon juice and rinse two or three times to prevent injury to the fabric.

GREASE STAINS

Wagon grease or tar spots should be rubbed well with lard or kerosene while the grease is fresh. Let the lard remain a while, then wash out in cold, soft water, using no soap.

TO CLEAN CORSETS

Take out the steels at front and sides, then scrub thoroughly with tepid or cold lather of white Castile soap, using a very small scrubbing brush. Do not lay them in water. When quite clean, let cold water run on them freely from the spigot to rinse out the soap thoroughly. Dry, without ironing (after pulling lengthwise until they are straight and shapely), in a cool place.

FURNITURE POLISH

One tablespoonful sweet oil; one tablespoonful lemon juice; one tablespoonful cornstarch.

HOME REMEDIES

CURES FOR HOUSEHOLD PESTS

Rats are said to have such a dislike for potash, that if it is powdered and scattered around their haunts, they will leave them. A piece of rag well soaked in a solution of cayenne is a capital thing to put into rat and mice holes as they will not attempt to eat it. A plug of wood, covered with a piece of flannel so prepared may be used to fill up the holes. Cockroaches and ants have a similar dislike of cayenne and a little strewed about a cellar will keep it clear of them.

ANT REPELLANT

Oil of sassafras dropped on shelves will drive away ants.

FLY REPELLANT

Branches of the elder bush hung in the dining room will clear it of flies. It has an odor which the insects detest.

GLASS CLEANER

Two or three tablespoons of coal oil in a half bucket of lukewarm water is good for cleaning window glass.

REMOVE INK

Sapolio will remove ink stains from china and the hand.

HOME REMEDIES

REMOVE SOOT STAINS

Perhaps it is not generally known that a cloth saturated with kerosene will speedily remove soot stains from the teakettle or other tin utensils.

CLEANING PORCELAIN

To clean the brown from porcelain kettle, boil peeled potatoes in it. The porcelain will be rendered nearly as white as when new.

DESTROY BAD SMELLS

To remove the smell of onions and other odors from utensils, put some wood ashes into the vessel, add boiling water and let it stand a short time on the back of the stove.

A little vinegar boiling in a vessel on the stove while onions are cooking will destroy much of the odor of onions.

TO CLEAN WATER BOTTLES

Put about two tablespoonfuls of vinegar to one of salt and shake round for a few minutes. Then rinse with clear water.

It (Willamette Valley) resembled an enchanted valley as we wound around the hill before descending it.
                                - Lucia Lorain Williams, 1851

INDEX OF RECIPES

PUTTING UP ON
THE TRAIL

HERITAGE COOKING

GERMAN

SWEDISH

DANISH

CZECH

POLISH

IRISH

HOME REMEDIES

CONCOCTIONS FOR AILMENTS

BEAUTY REGIMENS

THE PERFECT GIFT

The Oregon Trail Cookbook is perfect for all cooks, history buffs and collectors. Return an order form and your check or money order to:

Oregon Trail Cookbook
Morris Publishing
P.O. Box 233
Kearney, NE 68848

Please mail me _____ copies of the Oregon Trail Cookbook at $10.95 per copy and $2.00 for shipping and handling for each book. Nebraska residents add state tax of 5% and any local tax on your total order. Enclosed is my check or money order for $ _____ .

Mail Books To: (Please type or print)

     NAME _____

     ADDRESS _____

     CITY _____ **STATE** _____ **ZIP** _____

Please mail me _____ copies of the Oregon Trail Cookbook at $10.95 per copy and $2.00 for shipping and handling for each book. Nebraska residents add state tax of 5% and any local tax on your total order. Enclosed is my check or money order for $ _____ .

Mail Books To: (Please type or print)

     NAME _____

     ADDRESS _____

     CITY _____ **STATE** _____ **ZIP** _____

Please mail me _____ copies of the Oregon Trail Cookbook at $10.95 per copy and $2.00 for shipping and handling for each book. Nebraska residents add state tax of 5% and any local tax on your total order. Enclosed is my check or money order for $ _____ .

Mail Books To: (Please type or print)

     NAME _____

     ADDRESS _____

     CITY _____ **STATE** _____ **ZIP** _____